Le Rouvray

Diane de Obaldia,
with Marie-Christine Flocard
and Cosabeth Parriaud

Neptune Basin at Versailles

❧ Credits

Editor-in-Chief	Barbara Weiland
Technical Editor	Kerry I. Hoffman
Managing Editor	Greg Sharp
Copy Editor	Liz McGehee
Proofreaders	Tina Cook, Leslie Phillips
Text and Cover Designer	David Chrisman
Typesetter	Shean Bemis
Photographer	Brent Kane
Illustrator	André Samson
Cover Illustrator	Thomas Boatman

Obaldia, Diane de,
   Le Rouvray / Diane de Obaldia with Marie-
Christine Flocard and Cosabeth Parriaud.
        p.   cm. — (International quilt shop series)
      Includes bibliographical references.
      ISBN 1-56477-066-4
      1. Rouvray (Shop : Paris, France) 2. Patchwork—
France—Patterns. 3. Quilting—France—
Patterns. 4.   Patchwork quilts—France.
   I. Flocard, Marie-Christine. II. Parriaud, Cosabeth.
   III. Title. IV. Series.
TT835.023   1994
746.46—dc20   94-29984
                                                                  CIP

❧ Mission Statement

We are dedicated to providing quality products that encourage creativity and promote self-esteem in our customers and our employees.

We strive to make a difference in the lives we touch.

That Patchwork Place is an employee-owned, financially secure company.

❧ Le Rouvray ©

Printed in Hong Kong
99 98 97 96 95 94   6 5 4 3 2 1

❧ Acknowledgments

Our heartfelt thanks to the entire staff of Le Rouvray, who enthusiastically participated in this book by contributing the projects and stories herein.

Thanks also go to our clients, who bring us inspiration every day.

To the editors of That Patchwork Place, we express our appreciation for their confidence in selecting Le Rouvray as one of the first European shops in the International Quilt Shop Series.

Long live the passion we all share.

Table of Contents

Le Rouvray and I

A quilt shop in Paris, France, practically next door to Notre Dame cathedral! Nothing was further from my mind as I grew up in Michigan.

My mother made my clothes and taught me sewing, and during the long, hot Tennessee summers, my grandmother showed me the basics of patchwork and quilting. Later, these quiet occupations were not my

priorities as I set out for great adventures.

After a detour via the University of Michigan and then the fashion office of Marshall Fields in Chicago, I finally arrived at my dreamed-of destination . . . Paris! Fun and glamour were provided as I worked as a model in the French haute couture at such prestigious establishments as Chanel, Pierre Cardin, and Dior.

Then, marriage to a French "country gentleman" introduced me to château life in Normandy. Near the

château was a beautiful fortified farm surrounded by moats. The building was very old—dating back to the Hundred Years' War between France and England. The name of the farm—Le Rouvray—is derived from the medieval French word *rouvre*, which means 'oak'.

I didn't know it at the time, but this would be the birthplace of the quilt shop that is now located in Paris. Decorator friends in Chicago wanted me to find French antiques in the Norman countryside so I opened an antique shop at Le Rouvray, a two-hour drive from Paris. With only a small collection of armoires and buffets, the walls looked rather bare. I decided to bring a few quilts from the United States to

decorate them. The quilts drew the most attention. I was soon running back and forth between Paris and Le Rouvray in an old van loaded with quilts. As we chugged past Chartres cathedral, my daughter Sylvie, then three years old, would often be curled up and sleeping among the quilts.

It was about that time that the Jonathan Holstein quilt collection, sponsored by the Whitney Museum, came to the Musée des Arts Décoratifs in Paris. It was time for Le Rouvray to go to Paris. With a stroke of luck, I found a shop in a seventeenth-century building on the picturesque Left Bank of the Seine. Overhead beams, ancient tile floors, and small windowpanes gave the place great charm and made a perfect background for quilts.

Atmosphere was added by the neighborhood itself. Situated in the heart of Paris, surrounded by narrow streets, book stalls, and nearby houseboats moored on the banks of the Seine, it couldn't have been more perfect, and it is still our home.

Le Rouvray in Paris began with a collection of 200 antique quilts and a selection of "early-American" furniture. In fact, the pine pieces were from England but the overall look was "Americana." Success with the press and the public was immediate. Soon, the American embassy in Paris contacted me. They asked me to lend a collection of thirty antique quilts for a cultural tour of France. The show traveled to museums throughout France for two years.

I often went along, discovering places I hadn't visited before and carrying the quilting message, which was spreading like wildfire.

Now, twenty years later, quilting is "on the map" in France. The English word "patchwork" has been adopted and describes anything from a political meeting (patchwork of ideas) to a quilt. At Le Rouvray, we feature many classes, directed by two top teachers (my co-authors) and by visiting teachers. Our dynamic and multinational staff consists of dedicated quilters. A quilting thread that has found its way into someone's sandwich is a common occurrence at lunchtime. Hardly a day passes when we don't see an imaginative project made by a staff member or client. The shop is bursting with fabrics, supplies, and books. We would push the walls back if we could! Quilters visiting Paris usually find their way to Le Rouvray and we hope you will too. Please come to visit us soon. Even if you don't speak French, we speak Patchwork fluently!

Diane de Obaldia

My Co-Authors

One is blond and the other brunette; beyond that striking difference, Marie-Christine Flocard and Cosabeth Parriaud have parallels in their lives.

Standing, left to right: Viviane Martin-Schloesing, Joëlle de Bailliencourt, Jeanne Chausson, Inès Travers, Christine Meynier, Soizik Labbens, Cosabeth Parriaud, Marie-Christine Flocard, Vanessa Gouju, Renée Gosse, Annick Huet, Willemke Vidinic, Marie-Paule Mariani. Sitting, left to right: Marie-Claude Gaillochet, Liesbeth Lafarge, Diane de Obaldia (shop owner), Jacqueline Billion.

They met each other at Le Rouvray, where they are the guiding lights of our teaching staff. Although they're both French, they might have met in California—they both began quilting in San Francisco at the same time in the late 1970s. They are both married to charming and supportive husbands; both have two children; both are great cooks as well as wonderful teachers and textile artists.

As the three of us worked together on this book—writing, translating, organizing, and checking each detail and measurement—we decided we were as much co-ordinators as authors. In fact, there are numerous authors. Each staff member contributed a project and has told her "quilt story," which is also part of the story of Le Rouvray and of quilting in France—a story that unfolds each day.

Jouy 1993

I am lucky to live in Jouy en Josas, a charming village near Versailles, where Christophe-Philippe Oberkampf began printing the famous toiles de Jouy (printed fabrics) in 1760.

Musée Municipal de la Toile de Jouy

In 1992, after visiting the Musée Municipal de la Toile de Jouy near my home, I had the idea of using these very special fabrics in one of my quilts. A few days later, another "crazy" idea came to me. Why not organize a national French competition and exhibit projects combining patchwork and toiles de Jouy? As a member of the board of the French Patchwork Guild, I introduced the idea at our next meeting. Everyone was enthusiastic, and the unanimous decision was to try to make it happen. Two weeks later, I met with the museum's curator, who offered her beautiful location for the exhibit, which was scheduled for 1994. She explained to me that she did not know how many of these famous "Toiles" were still printed and suggested that I visit all the fabric editors (manufacturers) who might still be producing them. In addition, we decided that the condition for entry in the contest would be that one-third of each quilt had to include toile de Jouy fabrics.

Six months later, I had collected a sample of every design still being printed and had verified their accuracy with the museum documents. The published list includes fifty-one toiles designed in the eighteenth and nineteenth centuries by Manufacture Oberkampf and still printed in France. All of them are included in my quilt: Jouy 1993.

There are eighty-three hexagons and ten half hexagons in this quilt. All of the centers are different because I used samples of toiles that I had collected to prepare the exhibit "Patchworks and Toiles de Jouy," which took place from March to June 1994 at the museum in Jouy en Josas.

Marie-Christine Flocard

Jouy 1993, by Marie-Christine Flocard, 1993, les Loges en Josas, France, 63¾" x 52½". This quilt is truly a sampler: 93 different samples of toiles were used to make the hexagons and half-hexagons. Machine pieced and hand quilted.

Below are pillows made with toiles. Kits may be ordered from Le Rouvray. See page 94.

7

❦ Quilt size: 62¾" x 52½"

Finished block size: 7" (from point to point across the center of the hexagon block)

❦ Materials: 44"-wide fabric

¼ yd. each of 8 different large-scale prints for hexagon centers*
⅜ yd. blue solid for logs and inner border
⅝ yd. green solid for logs and inner border
1¼ yds. red solid for logs, binding, and border corners
1⅝ yds. off-white for logs and middle border
¼ yd. large-scale print (or toile de Jouy) for outer border*
1½ yds. beige for backing
60" x 70" piece of thin batting

*Yardage listed above for the hexagon centers and the outer border is for 44"-wide fabrics. The toile de Jouy fabrics are printed in different widths (40", 52", and 56"). American home-decorating fabrics range from 54"–60" wide. Adjust the yardage accordingly if you use these fabrics.

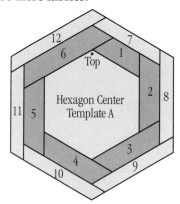

Block #1
Finished size: 7"
(from top point to bottom point)
Make 83.

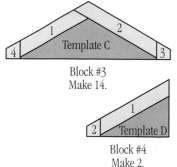

Template C
Block #3
Make 14.

Template D
Block #4
Make 2.
Make 2 reversed.

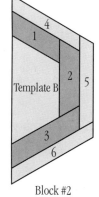

Template B
Block #2
(half-hexagon)
Make 10.

❦ Cutting

Templates are on page 12.

From the **large-scale prints** (or toiles), cut:

83 pieces each, using Template A. To center the fabric motif, move the template around on your fabric before tracing the hexagon onto the wrong side of the fabric. Mark the top point of the hexagon as indicated on the template.

6 strips, each 1¾" x 42", for outer border

From the **blue solid,** cut:

18 strips, each 1¼" x 42", for the first row of logs

4 Template C for Block #3 (top and bottom triangles)

1 Template D for Block #4 (corner triangle)

1 Template D reversed for Block #4 (corner triangle)

2 strips, each 1¼" x 42", for inner left side border

From the **green solid,** cut:

18 strips, each 1¼" x 42", for the first row of logs

4 Template C for Block #3 (top and bottom triangles)

1 Template D for Block #4 (corner triangle)

1 Template D reversed for Block #4 (corner triangle)

2 strips, each 1¼" x 42", for inner right side border

From the **red solid,** cut:

19 strips, each 1¼" x 42", for the first row of logs

6 Template C for Blocks #3

4 Template E for border corners

6 strips, each 1¼" x 42", for straight-grain binding

From the **off-white,** cut:

57 strips, each 1" x 42", for the second row of logs

6 strips, each 1" x 42", for middle border

Making the Blocks

Use accurate ¼"-wide seam allowances. Refer to the block plans for the piecing sequence.

BLOCK #1 (Hexagon blocks)

Step 1. Group together the hexagon centers (Template A) with color strips for the first row of logs. In 27 of the blocks, the first-row logs are red, in 28 they are green, and in 28 they are blue.

Step 2. With right sides together, stitch log #1 in place as shown. Press the seam, then trim the excess fabric as shown.

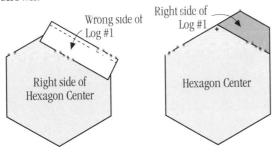

Step 3. Add the remaining first-row logs (#2–#6) in numerical order, pressing and trimming after each addition.

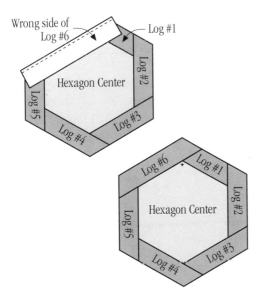

Step 4. Beginning with log #7, stitch the second row of logs (off-white) in place, in the same manner as the first row.

BLOCK #2 (Half-hexagon blocks)

Step 1. Group together the half-hexagon centers (Template B) with blue and green strips for the first row of logs. In 5 of the blocks, the first-row logs are blue and in 5 they are green. The logs will be added to the short sides of the block.

Step 2. Stitch the first-row logs in place, then the second row of off-white logs in the same manner as Block #1.

BLOCK #3 (Top and bottom triangles)

Step 1. Stitch logs #1 and #2 (off-white) in order to triangles (Template C). Press the seams and trim the excess fabric after adding each log.

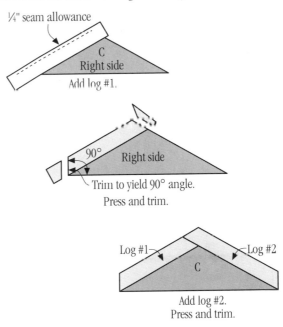

Step 2. Stitch logs #3 and #4 (off-white) in place. Press and trim.

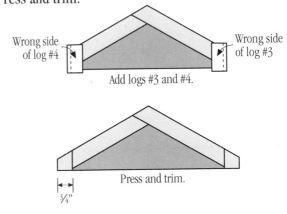

BLOCK #4

Stitch log #1 (off-white) to triangles (Template D). Press the seam and trim the excess fabric. Add log #2 (off-white). Press and trim.

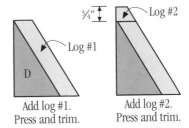

Jony 1993

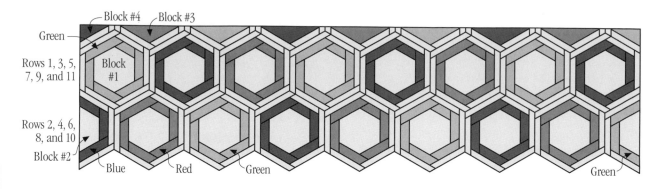

Block #4 — Block #3
Green —
Rows 1, 3, 5, 7, 9, and 11 — Block #1
Rows 2, 4, 6, 8, and 10 —
Block #2 —
Blue — Red — Green — Green

✏ Assembling the Quilt Top

Step 1. Arrange the completed blocks, referring to the color photo and to the illustration above. Note that horizontal rows 1, 3, 5, 7, 9, and 11 alternate green, blue, and red Blocks #1, in that order, from left to right. There are 8 blocks in each of these rows. Rows 2, 4, 6, 8, and 10 begin on the left side with a blue Block #2, then alternate red, green, and blue Blocks #1 across the width of the quilt. End the row with a green Block #2. There are 7 Blocks #1 and 2 Blocks #2 in these rows.

Step 2. Sew the blocks together in rows 1, 3, 5, 7, 9, and 11.

Step 3. Sew the blocks together in rows 2, 4, 6, 8, and 10.

Step 4. Sew Blocks #3 to the top of row 1. See "Set-in Seams" on pages 77–78 for directions to accurately insert triangles into inside corners.

Step 5. Stitch a Block #4 to the upper left corner of row 1 and a Block #4 reversed to the upper right corner.

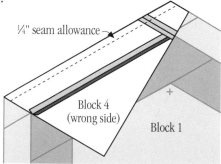

¼" seam allowance
Block 4 (wrong side)
Block 1

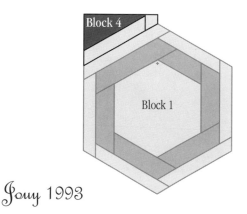

Block 4
Block 1

Step 6. Sew the rows of blocks together. Refer to the directions for "Set-in Seams" on pages 77–78.

Step 7. Stitch the remaining Blocks #3 in place on the bottom of row 11 as you did to the top of row 1 in step 4.

Step 8. Stitch a Block #4 to the lower left corner of row 11 and a Block #4 reversed to the lower right corner.

Step 9. Add the borders, measuring and cutting as directed for borders with straight-cut corners on page 87. Piece the blue inner left side border strips end to end. Piece the green inner right side border strips end to end. Sew the blue strips to the left side and the green strips to the right side. Press the seams.

Step 10. Measure the quilt top again, including the inner borders. Piece the 1"-wide off-white middle border strips end to end as necessary. Piece the 1¾"-wide large-scale print outer border strips end to end as necessary.

Step 11. Sew the middle and outer border strips together along the long sides and treat as one border strip. Make 2 pieced strips for the top and bottom. Make 2 pieced strips for the sides. Press seams toward the outer border.

Step 12. Sew the top and bottom borders to the quilt. Press seam toward the quilt.

Step 13. Stitch the red corner squares (Template E) to each end of the side border strips. Sew the side border strips to the quilt.

✏ Finishing the Quilt

Step 1. Layer the quilt top with batting and backing; baste. Quilt as desired.

Step 2. Bind the edges with the straight-grain strips of red solid fabric. (See page 92.)

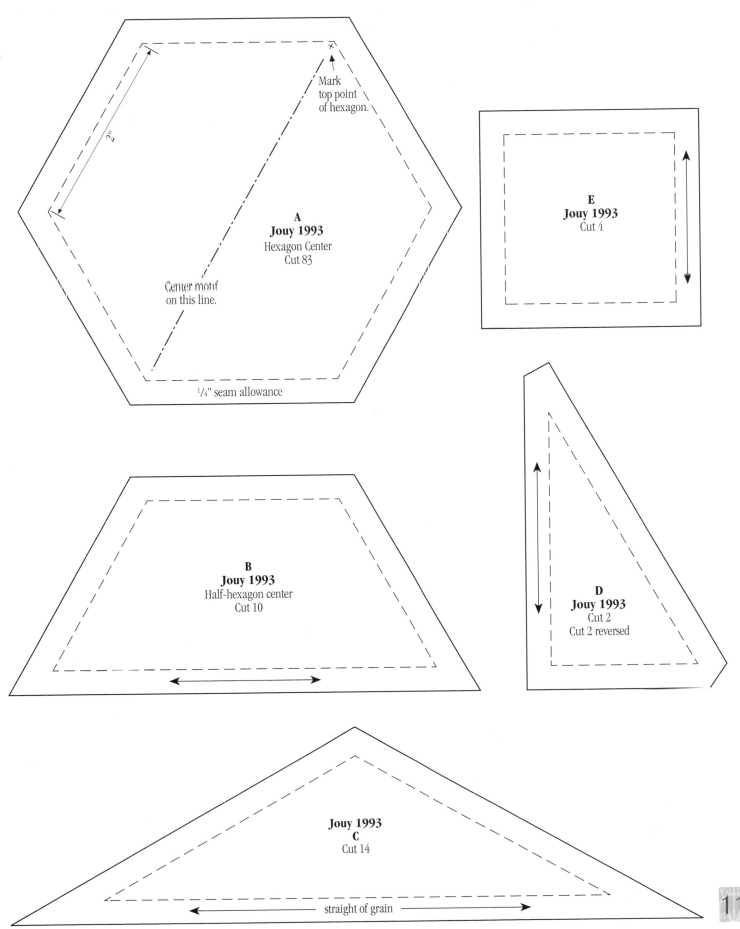

Mark top point of hexagon.

2"

A
Jouy 1993
Hexagon Center
Cut 83

Center motif on this line.

¹/₄" seam allowance

E
Jouy 1993
Cut 4

B
Jouy 1993
Half-hexagon center
Cut 10

D
Jouy 1993
Cut 2
Cut 2 reversed

Jouy 1993
C
Cut 14

straight of grain

The History of the Toiles de Jouy

In 1760 Christophe-Philippe Oberkampf, who was a dyer and an engraver, created a textile mill in the small village of Jouy en Josas (near Versailles).

White fabrics were imported from India and Switzerland, then dyed with plant dyes and printed with wood blocks, copper plates, or copper rolls (cylinders) at Oberkampf Manufacture. To qualify for the mill trademark of "bon teint" (dye-fast), the fabric had to go through a high-quality, multiple-step dyeing process. Oberkampf soon became a Royale Manufacture (official fabric printer to the royal court). At its peak in 1790, more than 1300 workers (530 of whom were women) were employed by Oberkampf. After 1806, the mill began to falter due to increased competition in France and to a blockade Great Britain imposed on French imports. Oberkampf Manufacture closed in 1843.

The term "toiles de Jouy" is generally associated only with Oberkampf Manufacture's prints that typically illustrate either rural or pastoral life of the late eighteenth century or scenes from antiquity. In addition to these prints, Oberkampf Manufacture is well known for the polychrome floral prints that were an important part of their production. Both fabric genres were used for decorating and clothing.

Many of the original designs are still printed and sold, using blocks and copper rolls that were acquired when the Oberkampf mill closed. They are printed by some of the most famous French fabric editors, such as Braquenié, Burger, Comoglio, Frey, Hamot, Lelièvre, Le Manach, Nobilis Fontan, and Prelle.

Summertime in Deauville, by Liesbeth Lafarge, 1987, Coye la Forêt, France, 36¼" x 58¾". Hand pieced and hand quilted.

Summertime in Deauville
(Eté à Deauville)

Several years ago, my family and I spent our summer vacation near Deauville, which is on the Normandy coast. Before we went, a friend and I had taken our first quilting lesson at Le Rouvray. Like all beginners, we started by assembling triangles and squares. The second lesson was scheduled to take place after the summer holidays.

As I was relaxing in the sun on the famous Deauville beach near the boardwalks, I came across a photo of a geometric quilt in a magazine. I loved it and decided to immediately start a small bed quilt. My daughters and some of their friends became interested and sewed some of the squares. The results weren't always perfect, but now we remember pleasant hours in blue and white surroundings—sailboats, white clouds, houses, and the blue sky and sea. Some months later, after my second quilting lesson, I was able to complete "Summertime in Deauville."

Liesbeth Lafarge

The boardwalk in Deauville attracts movie stars, society matrons, and others who flock to this popular seaside playground.

13

🐚 Quilt size: 36¼" x 58¾"

Finished block size: 3¾" x 3¾"

🐚 Materials: 44"-wide fabric

1½ yds. white
1¾ yds. blue
1¾ yds. for backing

This quilt is made with two different blocks. Make 68 of Block #1 and 67 of Block #2.

Block #1
Finished size: 3¾" x 3¾"
Make 68.

Block #2
Finished size: 3¾" x 3¾"
Make 67.

The directions that follow are for rotary cutting. For template cutting, use the templates on page 15.

🐚 Cutting

Cut all strips across the fabric width (crosswise grain). From the **white** fabric, cut:

5 strips, each 3⅛" wide; crosscut into 3⅛" x 3⅛" squares. You need a total of 68 squares for Blocks #1. If necessary, cut 3–6 additional squares instead of cutting an extra strip. (Or cut 68 Template A.)

6 strips, each 4¼" wide; crosscut into 1¾" x 4¼" rectangles. You need a total of 134 white rectangles for Blocks #2. If necessary, cut 2–4 additional rectangles instead of cutting an extra strip. (Or cut 134 Template C.)

From the **blue** fabric, cut:

9 strips, each 2¾" wide; crosscut into 2¾" x 2¾" squares. Cut each square once diagonally to yield 2 triangles. You need a total of 136 squares to make 272 triangles for Blocks #1. If necessary, cut 3–6 additional triangles instead of cutting an extra strip.(Or cut 272 Template B.)

3 strips, each 4¼" wide; crosscut into 1¾" x 4¼" rectangles. You need a total of 67 blue rectangles for Blocks #2. If necessary, cut 2–4 additional rectangles instead of cutting an extra strip.

5 strips, each 1¾" wide, for borders

5 strips, each 1¼" wide, for straight-grain binding

🐚 Assembling the Quilt Top

Use accurate ¼"-wide seam allowances.

Step 1. Piece Blocks #1 and #2 as shown.

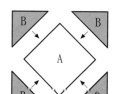 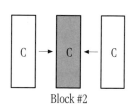

Block #1   Block #2

Step 2. Arrange the blocks, alternating Blocks #1 and #2 as shown on the Quilt Plan on page 15. Sew the blocks together in 9 rows of 15 blocks each. Press the seams in opposite directions from row to row.

Step 3. Join the rows, making sure to match the seams between the blocks.

Step 4. Add the borders, measuring and cutting as directed for straight-cut corners on page 87. Stitch border strips together to equal the measurements of the quilt top. Stitch the borders to the sides, then to the top and bottom edges of the quilt top.

🐚 Finishing the Quilt

Step 1. Layer the quilt top with batting and backing; baste. Quilt as desired or follow the quilting suggestion.

Step 2. Bind the edges with the straight-grain strips of blue fabric. (See page 92.)

14

Quilting Suggestion

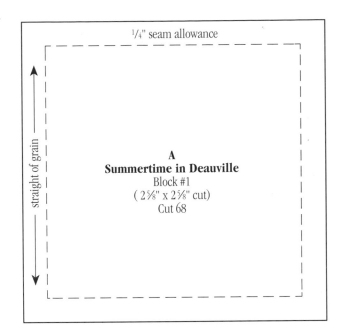

¹/₄" seam allowance

A
Summertime in Deauville
Block #1
(2⅝" x 2⅝" cut)
Cut 68

straight of grain

B
Summertime in Deauville
Block #1
Cut 272

Quilt Plan

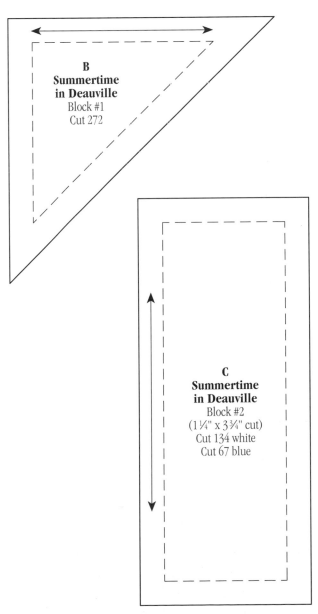

C
Summertime in Deauville
Block #2
(1¼" x 3¾" cut)
Cut 134 white
Cut 67 blue

Summertime in Deauville

Log Cabin by the Ocean
(Le log cabin au bord de l'océan)

For one-third of the year, I live and pursue quiltmaking in a small house by the ocean in Brittany, the westernmost part of France. My studio has a large window with a wonderful view of the Atlantic Ocean. The beautiful surroundings of Britanny have inspired a number of my quilts, including this one.

The rest of the year and between teaching engagements, I live in Nantes, a city in Brittany. Once, while I was there, I found a wonderful marbleized fabric in a shop that specializes in upholstery fabrics. Although it was rather heavy, it contained all the colors of Brittany—different shades of blue (sky and ocean), the rust and gold of the rocks, and a burgundy color that is reminiscent of some of the seaweeds that wash up onto the beach.

I decided to make a very simple quilt with just two fabrics. The colors in my marbleized ocean fabric were a perfect complement to a heavy off-white fabric that I liked. The Log Cabin Barn Raising block was a natural choice for me because it reminded me of the *petite maison bretonne* (small house in Brittany) where I was born.

Soizik
Labbens

Log Cabin by the Ocean, by Soizik Labbens, 1993, Nantes, France, 60" x 60". Two unusual decorator-style fabrics were used to make the Log Cabin blocks, which are arranged in a Barn Raising setting. Machine pieced and machine quilted.

🐚 Quilt size: 60" x 60"

Finished block size: 8¼" x 8¼"

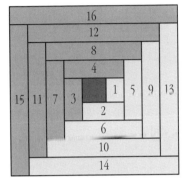

Log Cabin Block
Finished size: 8¼" x 8¼"
Make 36.

🐚 Materials

60"-WIDE DECORATOR FABRIC*

1¾ yds. marbleized decorator-style fabric
1½ yds. off-white fabric

44"- WIDE FABRIC

½ yd. gold for chimneys and inner border
½ yd. burgundy for chimneys and binding
⅛ yd. or scraps of teal blue for chimneys
4 yds. for backing
4½ yds. lightweight cotton flannel or muslin for block foundations and border interlining

*Yardage is based on 60"-wide American home-decorating fabrics, which range from 54"–60" wide. Adjust the yardage when using other widths of these fabrics. European decorator fabrics range in width from 40"–59". Prewashing decorator fabrics alters their appearance and finish. The yardage for this quilt is based on unwashed decorator fabrics. If you plan to launder your quilt, purchase additional fabric to allow for shrinkage.

🐚 Cutting

Cut border strips first, as directed below, to avoid having to piece the borders.

From the **marbleized** fabric, cut:

2 strips, each 4½" x 54", and 2 strips, each 4½" x 62", for outer border

24 strips, each 1½" x 60", for logs

From the **off-white** fabric, cut 24 strips, each 1½" x 60", for logs.

From the **gold** fabric, cut:

8 strips, each 1½" x 42", for inner border

1 strip, 1¾" x 21"; crosscut into 12 squares, each 1¾" x 1¾", for chimneys

From the **burgundy** fabric, cut:

12 squares, each 1¾" x 1¾", for chimneys
6 strips, each 1¼" x 42", for straight-grain binding

From the **teal blue** fabric, cut 12 squares, each 1¾" x 1¾", for chimneys.

From the **flannel** or **muslin**, cut:

2 strips, each 5½" x 54", for side borders

2 strips, each 5½" x 62", for top and bottom borders

36 squares, each 10" x 10", for foundation squares

🐚 Making the Blocks

Use ¼" seam allowances.

Step 1. With a pencil, draw 2 diagonal lines through each foundation square. Carefully center and pin the chimney in place as shown. Each corner of the chimney should touch one of the diagonal lines.

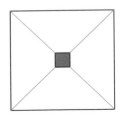

Log Cabin by the Ocean

Step 2. Pin an off-white strip on the right side of the chimney, right sides together. Stitch through all layers.

Trim strip here after stitching.

Step 3. Flip the strip onto the foundation. Trim the strip even with the chimney. Press.

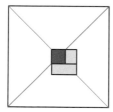

Step 4. In a clockwise direction, add another off-white strip in the same manner as you did in step 2. Flip the strip onto the foundation, trim even with the chimney, and press.

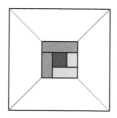

Step 5. Add marbleized fabric strips on the remaining 2 sides of the chimney as you did before.

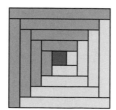

Step 6. Continue adding off-white and marbleized strips in a clockwise direction until you have 4 rows of each color. Make 36 blocks.

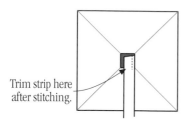

Make 36.

Assembling the Quilt Top

Step 1. Press and trim the excess foundation fabric from completed blocks. Trim to square up edges.

Step 2. Arrange the blocks as shown in the quilt plan below. Make sure you alternate chimney colors so that you do not have 2 chimneys of the same color next to each other.

Step 3. Sew the blocks together in 6 rows of 6 blocks each. Press the seams between each block.

Step 4. Sew the rows together, making sure to match the seams between each block.

Step 5. Add the borders, measuring and cutting as directed for straight-cut corners on page 87. Stitch gold border strips together to equal the measurements of the quilt top. Sew the 2 shorter gold inner border strips to the 2 shorter marbleized outer border strips. Do the same with the longer strips. You will then have only 4 multiple fabric border strips.

Step 6. Place the flannel strips on the wrong side of your border strips; pin or baste. Sew the top and bottom border strips to your quilt top, then add the side border strips.

Finishing the Quilt

Step 1. Layer the quilt top with the backing; baste. Machine quilt in-the-ditch around each block and around the inner border. Use invisible nylon thread for the top and a matching thread for the back.

Step 2. Bind the edges with the straight-cut strips of burgundy fabric. (See page 92.)

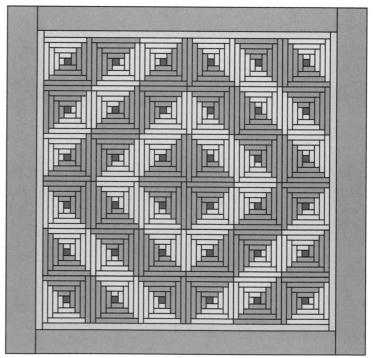

Quilt Plan

Log Cabin by the Ocean

Mountains in Corsica (Montagnes en Corse)

When I first saw a version of the Delectable Mountains pattern, my thoughts immediately turned to my native island of Corsica, mountains in the Mediterranean Sea. When I think about Corsica, I see images of beaches with a backdrop of rosy red rocks and large stands of umbrella pines ("Pinus pinea").

The French call Corsica the Isle of Beauty. To capture the true flavor of Corsica, you must leave the coast and take one of the narrow, winding roads up into the interior. Picturesque villages with sturdy, old granite houses and narrow streets are scattered on the wooded hillsides. The fragrance of the maquis, a flowering vegetation that exists here but not on the mainland, is unforgettable. Emperor Napoleon, a native of Corsica, remembered the fragrance of the Corsican maquis during the last days of his life when he was deported to the island of Saint Helen.

In the summer, if you hike on the trails leading to the high mountains, you walk alongside streams and often come upon *bergeries*. These are simple sheds occupied by shepherds, sheep, goats, pigs, and donkeys—alternately and sometimes simultaneously! At higher elevations, you find waterfalls and lakes surrounded by Corsican pines and by peaks that are covered with snow almost year 'round. Corsica is an island of a thousand wonders. It is a unique and special place.

Marie-Paule
Mariani

Mountains in Corsica, by Marie-Paule Mariani, 1985, Paris, France, 96" x 96". This striking red-and-white quilt is a variation of the traditional Delectable Mountains pattern. Hand pieced and hand quilted.

⚘ Quilt size: 96" x 96"

Finished block size: 10" x 10"

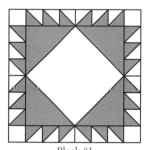

Block #1
Finished size: 10" x 10"
Make 25.

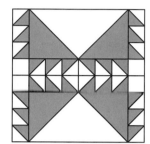

Block #2
Finished size: 10" x 10"
Make 40.

The directions that follow are for rotary cutting. For template cutting, use the templates on pages 21–22 and the fabric requirements indicated in parentheses below in the materials list.

⚘ Materials: 44"-wide fabric

9 yds. white for blocks and border (4½ yds. if using templates)

7½ yds. red for blocks and binding (4 yds. if using templates)

6 yds. white for backing

⚘ Cutting

Cut and reserve strips for the border.
From the **white** fabric, cut:

10 strips, each 3½" x 42", for border

BIAS SQUARES

Use accurate ¼"-wide seam allowances. Follow the directions on pages 78–79 to make bias squares.

Step 1. From the white and red fabrics, cut 15 pieces, each 12" x 42". From the pieces, cut 150 red strips and 150 white strips, each 1⅞" x 42".

Step 2. Sew the strips together in groups of 8, alternating 4 white and 4 red strips.

Step 3. Cut the strip-pieced segments 1¾" wide and the bias squares 1¾" x 1¾". You will need a total of 1560 white/red bias squares. (For template cutting, use Template B to cut 1560 each from white and red.)

Note: Press seams to the red side.

From the **white** fabric, cut:

11 strips, each 1¾" x 42"; crosscut into 260 squares, each 1¾" x 1¾". Use 100 squares for Blocks #1 and 160 squares for Blocks #2. (For template cutting, use Template A.)

5 strips, each 8¾" x 42"; crosscut into 20 squares, each 8¾" x 8¾". Cut each square twice diagonally to yield a total of 80 quarter-square triangles for Blocks #2. (For template cutting, use Template E.)

5 strips, each 5¾" x 42"; crosscut into 25 squares, each 5¾" x 5¾", for Block #1. (For template cutting, use Template D.)

16 squares, each 10½" x 10½", for the plain alternating blocks

From the **red** fabric, cut:

15 strips, each 4⅝" x 42"; crosscut into 130 squares, each 4⅝" x 4⅝". Cut each square once diagonally to yield a total of 260 half-square triangles. Use 100 triangles for Blocks #1 and 160 for Blocks #2. (For template cutting, use Template C.)

⚘ Assembling the Blocks and Quilt Top

Step 1. Follow the piecing sequence in the illustrations below and on page 21 to make Blocks #1 and #2. Press seams to the red side after stitching each seam.

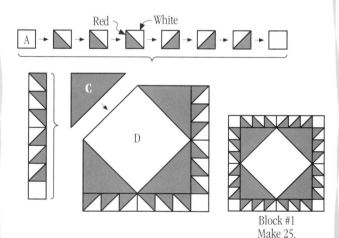

Block #1
Make 25.

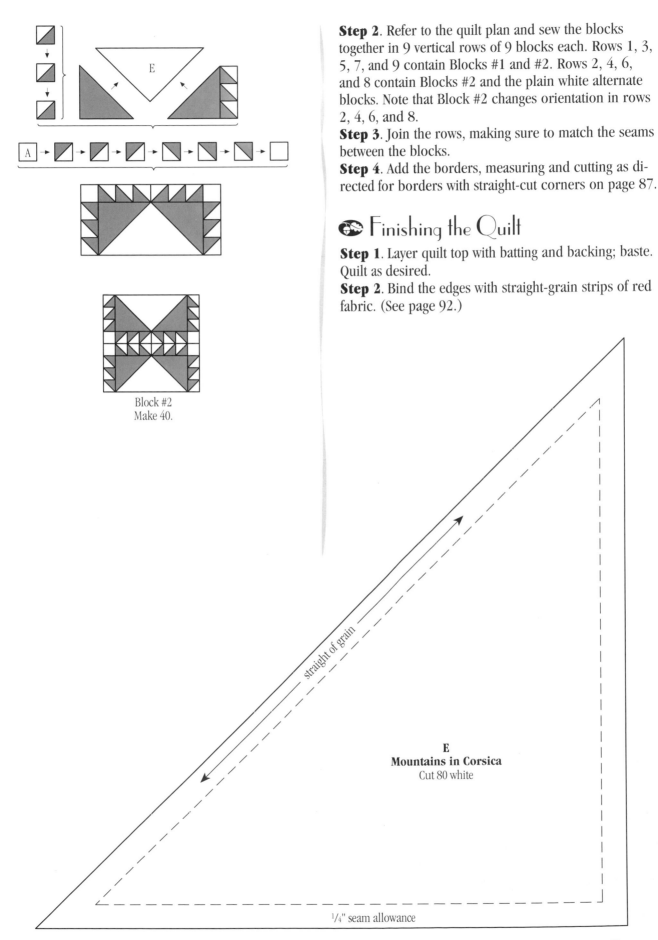

Step 2. Refer to the quilt plan and sew the blocks together in 9 vertical rows of 9 blocks each. Rows 1, 3, 5, 7, and 9 contain Blocks #1 and #2. Rows 2, 4, 6, and 8 contain Blocks #2 and the plain white alternate blocks. Note that Block #2 changes orientation in rows 2, 4, 6, and 8.

Step 3. Join the rows, making sure to match the seams between the blocks.

Step 4. Add the borders, measuring and cutting as directed for borders with straight-cut corners on page 87.

✦ Finishing the Quilt

Step 1. Layer quilt top with batting and backing; baste. Quilt as desired.

Step 2. Bind the edges with straight-grain strips of red fabric. (See page 92.)

Block #2
Make 40.

E
Mountains in Corsica
Cut 80 white

straight of grain

¼" seam allowance

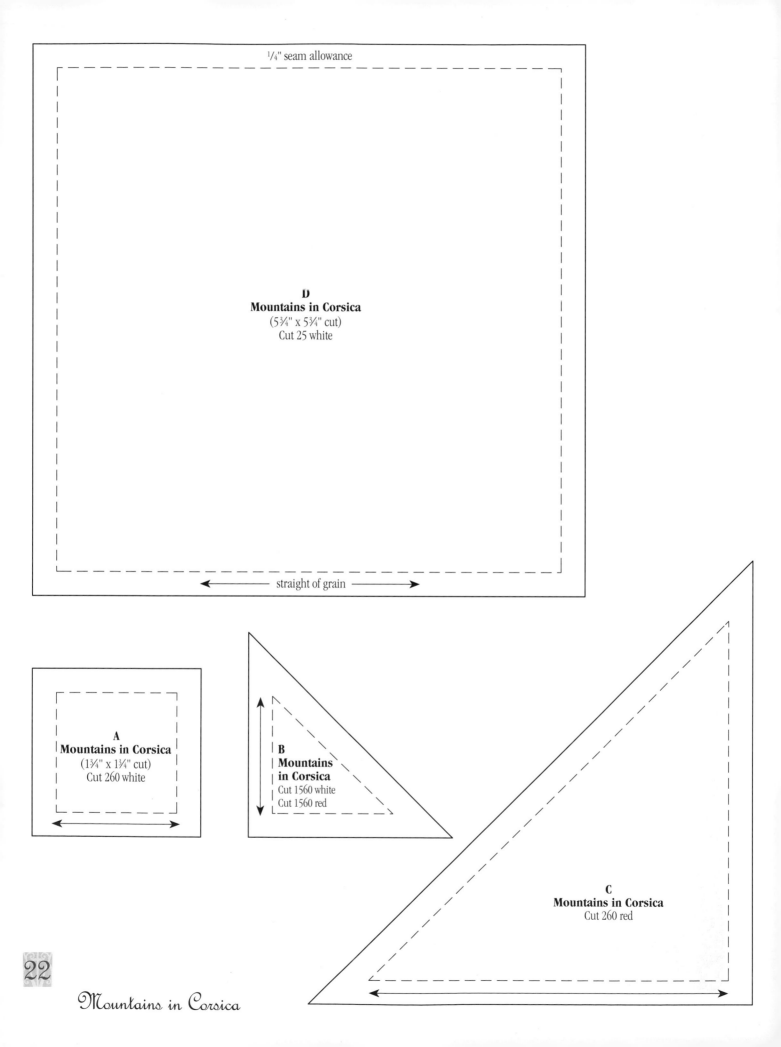

¼" seam allowance

D
Mountains in Corsica
(5¾" x 5¾" cut)
Cut 25 white

straight of grain

A
Mountains in Corsica
(1¾" x 1¾" cut)
Cut 260 white

B
Mountains in Corsica
Cut 1560 white
Cut 1560 red

C
Mountains in Corsica
Cut 260 red

Mountains in Corsica

Chartres Blues (Bleus de Chartres)

My architectural practice takes me three times weekly to Chartres. Needless to say, I am under the spell of the magnificient cathedral with its incomparable architecture and the mysterious light that filters through the stained-glass windows. Some of the blues are particularly intense and are referred to as "bleu de Chartres."

Inspired by the stained-glass windows, I wanted to reflect their colors in a geometric quilt that would make the transition from traditional to contemporary design. The solution was very simple. Traditional quilts (whether pieced or appliquéd) are often repetitions of identical blocks in which the colors and forms are always in the same place.

In my quilt, the basic form is a rectangle. However, I made each block look different enough so that unless you study the blocks closely, you don't immediately recognize that they are the same block. In each block, the length is equal to twice the width, so there are many possibilities for positioning the blocks.

At first glance, this quilt may look like a Crazy quilt, but look carefully. It is a composition of identical blocks like traditional quilts of the past. Once you've completed this project, you may approach quilt composition with a new perspective as I did, and as I try to teach my students to do in my classes on contemporary quilt design. The possibilities are infinite.

Jeanne Chausson

Chartres Blues, by Jeanne Chausson, 1986, Paris, France, 36" x 36". Hand pieced and hand quilted.

Quilt size: 36" x 36"

Finished block size: 3⅛" x 6¼"

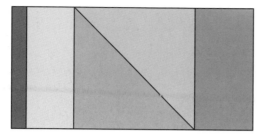

Chartres Blues Block
Finished size: 3⅛" x 6¼"
Make 32.

Materials: 44"-wide fabric

1⅜ yds. solid black for blocks, borders, and binding
¼ yd. each of 5 different blues, ranging from light to dark
⅛ yd. each (or scraps) of 3 different reds
1¼ yds. for backing

CUTTING

From the **black** fabric, cut:

    4 strips, each 1½" x 36"

    4 strips, each 3" x 36"

    32 Template A

    3 Template C

    2 Template D

    4 strips, each 1¼" x 42", for binding

From the **lightest blue** fabric, cut a total of 11 pieces:

    7 Template C

    2 Template B

    2 Template D

From the remaining 4 **blue** fabrics, cut a total of 103 pieces:

    26 Template B

    52 Template C

    25 Template D

From the 3 **red** fabrics, cut a total of 9 pieces:

    2 Template C

    4 Template B

    3 Template D

Making the Blocks

Piece each block as shown. Assemble the colors, following your own inspiration, or refer to the color photograph. Make 32 blocks.

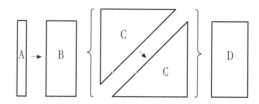

Assembling the Quilt Top

Step 1. Arrange the blocks in a way that pleases you or as shown. Jeanne clustered the blocks with red pieces (#12, #13, #15, #18, #19, #21, #22, and #28) in the center of the quilt.

Step 2. Sew the blocks together in sections as shown.

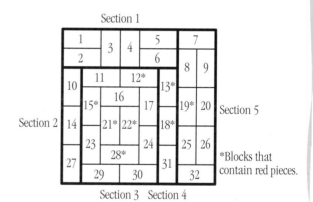

Step 3. Sew the sections together.

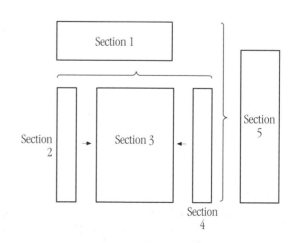

Chartres Blues

Adding the Borders

BORDER #1 (inner border)

Make a pieced inner border from blue and black strips. Measure the length and width of the quilt top as directed on page 87. Cut strips of varying lengths, each 1½" wide. Piece the strips together in random order to match the measurements. Sew the top and bottom borders onto the quilt top first, then add the side borders.

BORDER #2

Measure the length and width of the quilt top, including the inner border. From the black, cut 1½"-wide strips to match the measurements. Piece the strips as necessary to make the required lengths. Sew the top and bottom borders to the quilt top first, then add the side borders.

BORDER #3

Measure the quilt top as you did before, including borders #1 and #2. From one of the blue fabrics, cut 1½"-wide strips to match the measurements. Piece strips as necessary to make the required lengths. Sew the top and bottom borders to the quilt top first, then add the side borders.

BORDER #4

Measure the quilt top as you did before, including borders #1, #2, and #3. From the black, cut 3"-wide black strips to match the measurements, less the pieced squares, which will be stitched to each end of the side borders. Sew the top and bottom borders to the quilt top.

Piece scraps together to make 4 crazy-patch squares, each 3" x 3". After measuring the quilt top, stitch the pieced corner squares to each end of the side border strips. Sew the side borders to the quilt top.

Finishing the Quilt

Step 1. Layer the quilt top with batting and backing; baste.

Step 2. Quilt as desired.

Step 3. Bind the edges with straight-grain strips of the black solid fabric. (See page 92.)

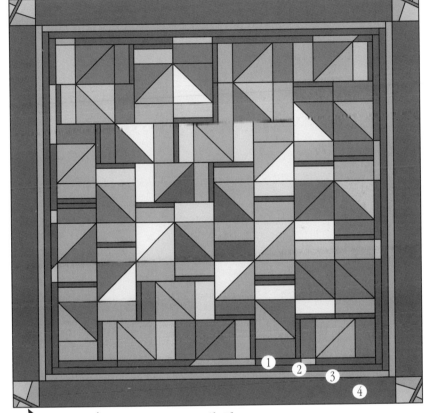

— Crazy-patch squares

Quilt Plan

Examples of crazy-patch squares.
Make four 3" x 3" squares.

Chartres Blues

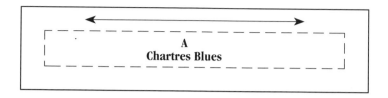

A
Chartres Blues

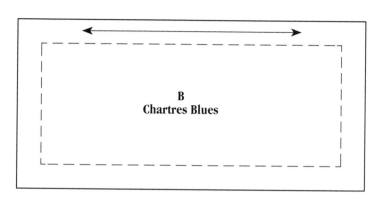

B
Chartres Blues

D
Chartres Blues

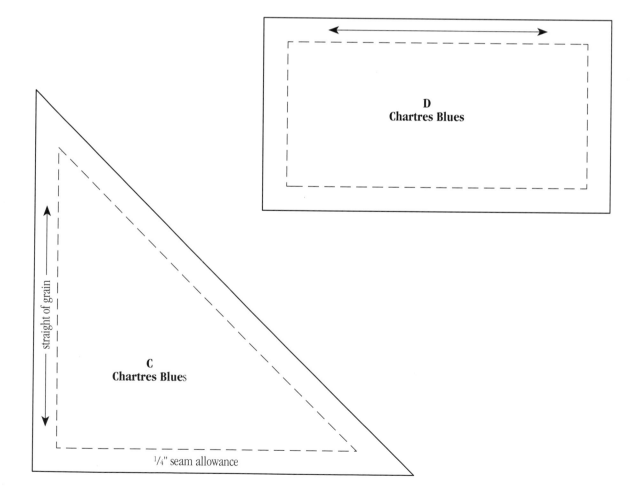

straight of grain

C
Chartres Blues

¹/₄" seam allowance

Chartres Blues

The Hamlet in Chantilly

(Le hameau de Chantilly)

I live in Chantilly, a beautiful town situated in the heart of an immense forest, thirty miles north of Paris. It is famous for its stables and racetrack. Eminent riders compete for the prestigious Prix de Diane or the Prix du Jockey Club awards. The people are very elegant, especially at the Prix de Diane, where the women wear haute couture fashions and wonderful hats.

Chantilly is also famous for its castle. In past centuries, there was a hamlet within the walls of the castle's park. Princes liked to visit the little cottages in the hamlet to rest and relax and escape the formalities of castle etiquette.

As the daughter of an architect, I have always loved houses and the variety of their styles. When I attended Cosabeth Parriaud's "Patchwork Houses" workshop at Le Rouvray, I made her simple Garden Houses block with my favorite floral fabric. I liked the block so much, I decided I wanted to make a bed quilt, but I had soon used all of the floral fabric and was unable to get more! I finished the quilt with three border strips in complementary fabrics and it worked. However, the moral of this story is that when you fall in love with a fabric, immediately buy at least two or three yards!

Marie-Claude Gaillochet

The Hamlet in Chantilly, by Marie-Claude Gaillochet, 1991, Chantilly, France, 62" x 86". Marie-Claude chose a floral-patterned fabric for the houses, to suggest countryside life. Hand pieced and hand quilted.

✺ Quilt size: 62" x 86"

Finished block size: 12" x 12"

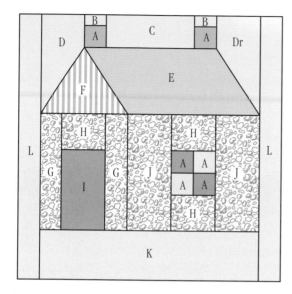

✺ Materials: 44"-wide fabric

1 yd. floral print for the house siding (Templates G, H, J)
¼ yd. dark pink for gables (Template F)
½ yd. light pink for roofs (Template E)
¼ yd. yellow for chimneys (Template A)
1 yd. light blue for windows (Template A), doors (Template I), and inner border
4 yds. white for windows (Template A), background (Templates B, C, D, D reversed, K, and L), and middle border
1⅓ yds. dark blue for outer border and binding
3½ yds. for backing

✺ Cutting

Use templates on pages 30–32.

From the **floral** print, cut:

30 Template G for siding
45 Template H for siding
30 Template J for siding

From the **dark pink** fabric, cut 15 Template F for gables.

From the **light pink** fabric, cut 15 Template E for roofs.

From the **yellow** fabric, cut 30 Template A for chimneys.

From the **light blue** fabric, cut:

4 strips, each 3" x 42", for side inner border*
2 strips, each 3" x 42", for top and bottom inner border*
30 Template A for windows
15 Template I for doors

From the **white** fabric, cut:

2 strips, each 7½" x 65½", for side middle border*
2 strips, each 7½" x 55½", for top and bottom middle border*
30 Template B for background
15 Template C for background
15 Template D for background
15 Template D reversed for background
15 Template K for background
30 Template L for background
30 Template A for windows

From the **dark blue**, cut:

4 strips, each 4" x 42", for side outer border
4 strips, each 4" x 42", for top and bottom outer border
8 strips, each 1½" x 42", for straight-grain binding

*Cut these strips before cutting template pieces.

Assembling the Quilt Top

Use accurate ¼"-wide seam allowances.

Step 1. Piece 15 blocks as shown. See directions for "Set-in Seams" on pages 77–78.

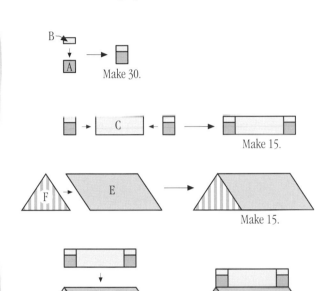

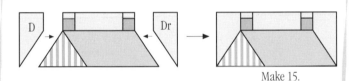

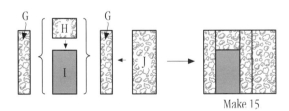

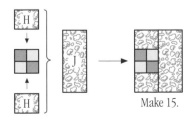

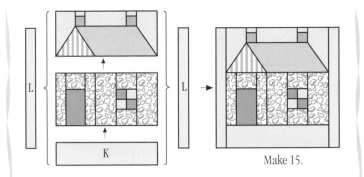

Make 15.

Step 2. Sew the blocks together in 5 rows of 3 blocks each, referring to the quilt plan on page 30.

Step 3. Add the borders, measuring and cutting as directed for borders with straight-cut corners on page 87. Stitch border strips together, if necessary, to equal the measurements of the quilt top. Add the light blue inner border first, then the white middle border, and finally the dark blue outer border.

Finishing the Quilt

Step 1. Layer the quilt top with batting and backing; baste. Quilt as desired or follow the quilting suggestion.

Step 2. Bind the edges with straight-grain strips of dark blue fabric. (See page 92.)

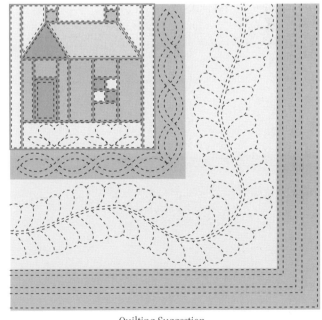

Quilting Suggestion

The Hamlet in Chantilly

Quilt Plan

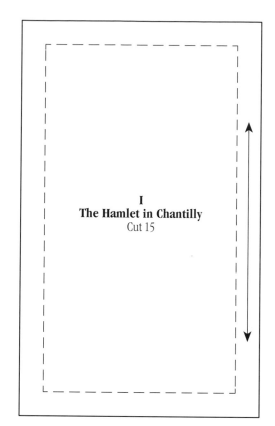

I
The Hamlet in Chantilly
Cut 15

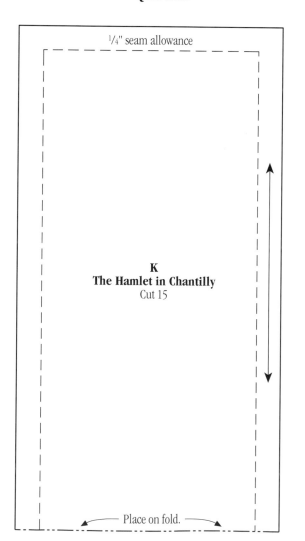

¹/₄" seam allowance

K
The Hamlet in Chantilly
Cut 15

← Place on fold. →

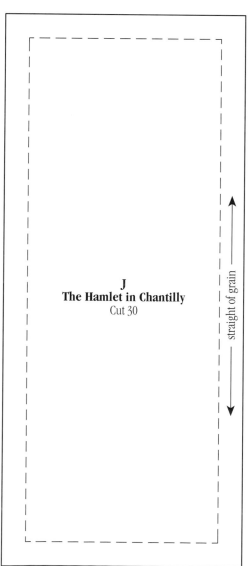

J
The Hamlet in Chantilly
Cut 30

straight of grain

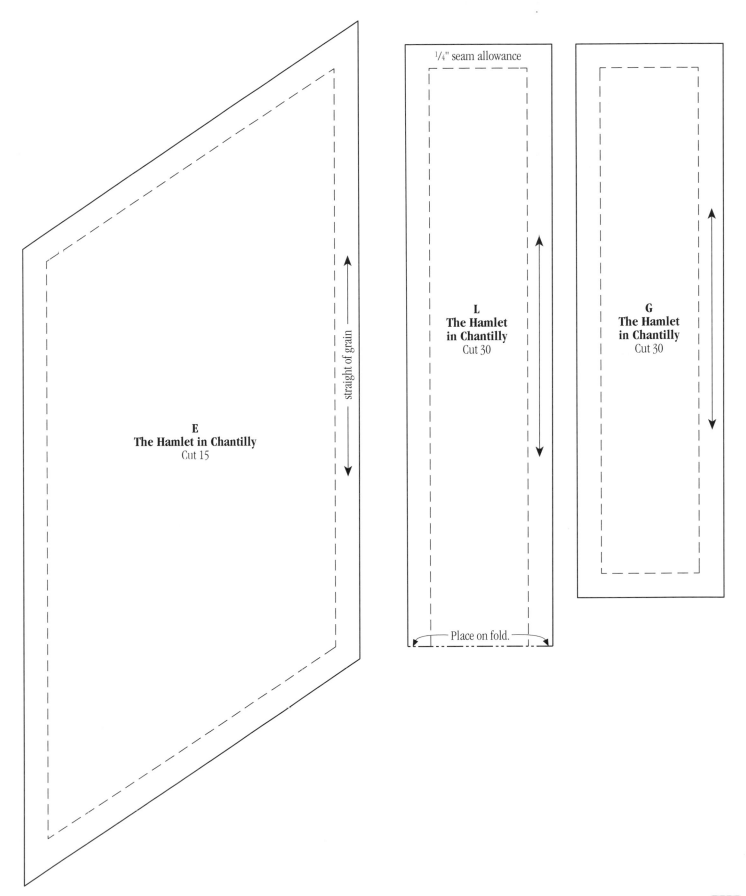

E
The Hamlet in Chantilly
Cut 15

straight of grain

¼" seam allowance

L
The Hamlet in Chantilly
Cut 30

Place on fold.

G
The Hamlet in Chantilly
Cut 30

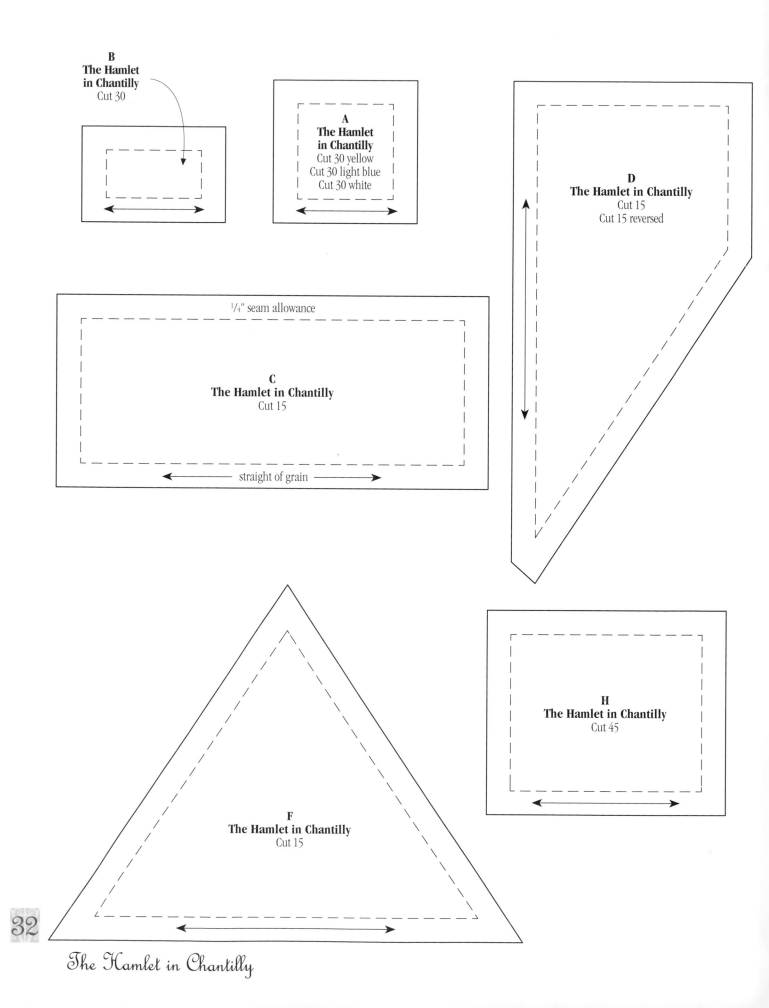

B
**The Hamlet
in Chantilly**
Cut 30

A
**The Hamlet
in Chantilly**
Cut 30 yellow
Cut 30 light blue
Cut 30 white

D
The Hamlet in Chantilly
Cut 15
Cut 15 reversed

¹/₄" seam allowance

C
The Hamlet in Chantilly
Cut 15

straight of grain

H
The Hamlet in Chantilly
Cut 45

F
The Hamlet in Chantilly
Cut 15

The Hamlet in Chantilly

Little Stars of Normandy

(Les petites étoiles normandes)

　　I was born in Normandy, near the historic city of Bayeux, famous for its ancient tapestry. The colors of the Norman landscapes change with the seasons, with the weather, and even with the hours of the day.

It was a challenge for me to capture the variety of these colors in eight-pointed, strip-pieced stars. However, like most Normans, I am tenacious and like challenges. As soon as I had finished the first star, I was very happy. The effect produced by the variety and color of the prints was what I had hoped for. For me, it was the essence of Normandy contained in an early-American quilt design.

　　Inès Travers

The choice of this American star pattern is appropriate because Inès was born only a few miles away from Omaha Beach, where the Americans landed on June 6, 1944 (D-day). The combination of plaid, striped, floral, checked, and solid fabrics make this quilt special, so be creative when you pull fabrics from your collection.

Little Stars of Normandy, by Inès Travers, 1993, Limours, France, 48½" x 48½". Hand and machine pieced; hand quilted.

33

🐞 Quilt size: 48½" x 48½"

Finished block size: 8⅛" x 8⅛"

Star Block
Finished size: 8⅛" x 8⅛"
Make 16.

🐞 Materials: 44"-wide fabric

2½ yds. total of assorted fabrics for the stars and
   binding*
2½ yds. off-white for background and borders
3 yds. for backing

*Inès used 70 different fabrics.

🐞 Cutting

From the **assorted** fabrics, cut:

   112 strips, each 1¼" x 42", for the stars

From the **off-white** fabric, cut:

   5 strips, each 2⅞" x 42"; crosscut into 64 squares,
      each 2⅞" x 2⅞" (or cut 64 Template B)

   2 strips, each 4⅝" x 42"; crosscut into 16 squares,
      each 4⅝" x 4⅝". Cut each square twice diago-
      nally to yield a total of 64 triangles (or cut 64
      Template C)

   2 strips, each 1¾" x 34½", for inner top and
      bottom border

   2 strips, each 1¾" x 38½", for inner side border

   2 strips, each 6½" x 38½", for outer top and
      bottom border

   4 strips, each 6½" x 42", for outer side border

🐞 Making the Blocks

Use accurate ¼"-wide seam allowances. Templates
are on page 36.

Step 1. Machine piece 7 of the 1¼"-wide strips
together, combining the strips in an order that is
pleasing. The strip set should be 5¾" wide. Make 16
sets of strips, each with a different combination of
fabrics.

Step 2. Cut 8 diamonds (Template A) from each of the
16 strip sets. Reserve the remaining portions of the strip
sets to make the middle border.

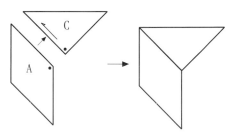

Strip 1
Strip 2
Strip 3
Strip 4
Strip 5
Strip 6
Strip 7

Strip Set

Step 3. For each block, sew a triangle to a diamond.
Begin stitching ¼" from the inner edge of the 2 pieces.
Stitch all the way to the outer edge.

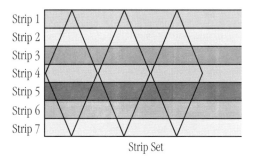

Step 4. Sew a second diamond to the triangle, starting
¼" inside the inner point. Stitch to the outer edge of the
pieces.

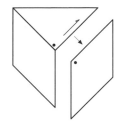

Step 5. Match the diamond points and sew them
together. Press this seam to one side and press the
triangle seams toward the diamonds. Make 4 for each
block.

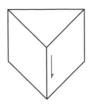

Step 6. Sew a square to a diamond unit. Start sewing at the outer edge and end the stitching ¼" from the inner edge.

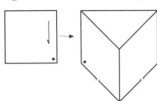

Step 7. Sew a second diamond unit to the square. Begin stitching ¼" from the inner point and stitch to the outer edge.

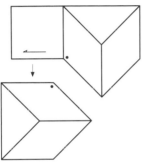

Step 8. Match the points of diamonds and sew them together. Press the seam in one direction. Press the seams between the square and diamond units toward the diamonds.

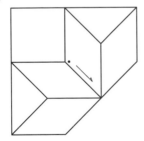

Step 9. Sew the edges of the diamond units to both edges of one square. Repeat with the remaining square.

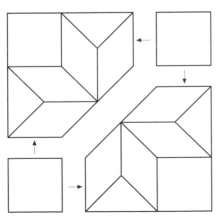

Sew center seam last.

Step 10. Match the center points and pin. Pull the corner square out of the way and stitch the two halves together through the center, from the inner point of one square to the inner point of the other square.

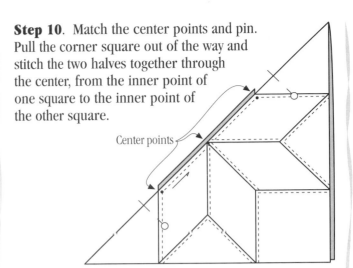

Center points

Step 11. Press center seam to one side. Press seams of the squares toward the diamonds.

ꙮ Assembling the Quilt Top

Step 1. Arrange the blocks in 4 rows of 4 blocks each.
Step 2. Sew the blocks together into rows, then sew the 4 rows together.
Step 3. Make the pieced middle border strips by cutting 1¼"-wide strips from the remaining portions of the strip units. Sew pieced strips together, end to end, to make 2 strips, each 34½" long, and 2 strips, each 38½" long.

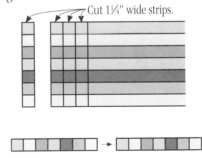

Cut 1¼" wide strips.

Step 4. Sew each of the pieced middle border strips to the off-white inner border strips of the same length.
Step 5. Add the borders to the quilt top, measuring and cutting as directed for borders with straight-cut corners on page 87. First add the top and bottom borders, then the side borders.
Step 6. Measure the quilt top, including the inner and middle borders. Stitch the white outer border strips together to equal the measurements. Sew the top and bottom borders to the quilt top, then add the side borders.

Little Stars of Normandy

Finishing the Quilt

Step 1. Layer the quilt top with batting and backing; baste.

Step 2. Quilt as desired.

Step 3. Bind the edges with varying lengths of straight-grain strips cut from different fabrics. (See page 92.)

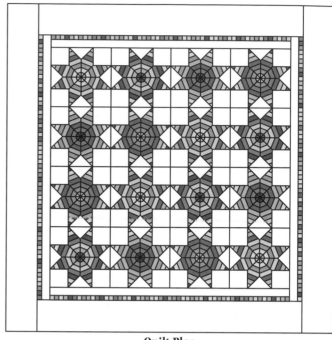

Quilt Plan

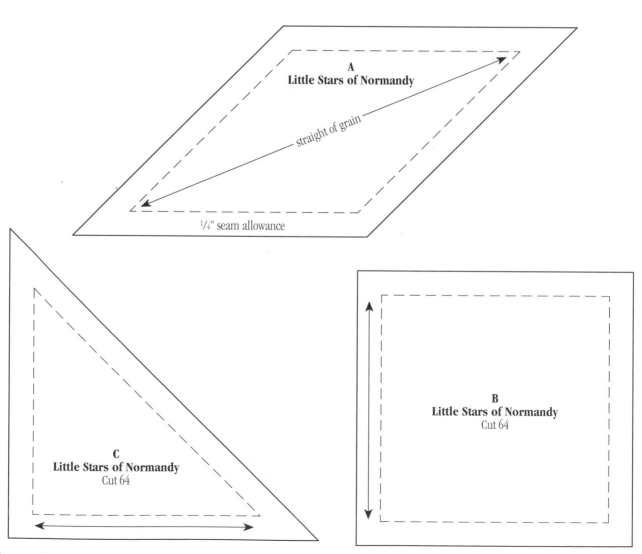

A
Little Stars of Normandy

straight of grain

¼" seam allowance

C
Little Stars of Normandy
Cut 64

B
Little Stars of Normandy
Cut 64

Little Stars of Normandy

Boutis Provençal Cradle Quilt

(Couverture de berceau en boutis provençal)

(Below)
Boutis Provençal Cradle Quilt, by Renée Gosse, 1992, Chatou, France, 20" x 22". Hand pieced and hand quilted.

I am from Provence, in the southern part of France, where sunshine, olive trees, the smell of lavender and thyme, and beautiful white counterpanes (bedcovers), which we call "Boutis provençaux," are all part of daily life.

My grandmother Catherine had a counterpane on every bed, and I have continued the tradition in my home. I have always owned several of these antique bedcovers, but I had never thought of making them myself.

One day, I visited a quilt exhibit of colorful patchworks. I stopped short in front of a large white nineteenth-century boutis. I was struck by the beauty and the simplicity of the whiteness amid the brightly colored patchworks. At home, I couldn't forget it and began searching for information. There wasn't much to be found and what I did find seemed incomplete, so one day I took my courage and my scissors in hand, and I picked apart a worn corner of an old boutis. Finally, I understood.

The boutis took me back to my origins—I was once again in Provence. What began as an adventure has become my passion. To date, I have made coverlets, bibs, bonnets, and baby coats. Through the classes I teach at Le Rouvray, I try to impart my enthusiasm and the secrets of an old French tradition.

Renée Gosse

The term "boutis" is used throughout the directions. It is a type of Marseilles white work. Similar to trapunto, boutis is also a stuffed quilting technique; however, contrary to trapunto, boutis is reversible.

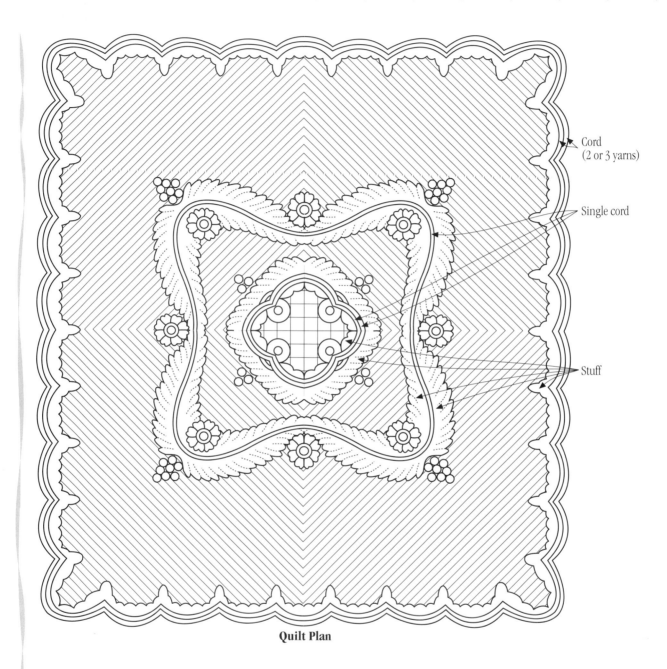

Cord
(2 or 3 yarns)

Single cord

Stuff

Quilt Plan

Materials: 44"-wide fabric

2 yds. of 100% white cotton fabric (unwashed)
100% cotton white thread
100% cotton knitting yarn for cording
Orange stick (manicure)
#18 blunt-tip tapestry needle
Trapunto needle
Approx. 1 yd. of thin, synthetic batting, cut into ¼" x 10" strips
14" quilting hoop

Quilt size: 20" x 22"

Cutting

From the **white** fabric, cut 2 rectangles, each 25¾" x 27¾".

Boutis Provençal

Preparing for Boutis

Use the pattern on the pullout pattern insert. The pattern is presented in a quadrant format.

Step 1. With a pencil, mark the exact center of one of the white rectangles. This will be point A. Using a long ruler, draw vertical and horizontal lines to divide the rectangle into quadrants as shown. These will be lines B. Next, divide each quadrant in half with 45° diagonal lines, which will be lines C.

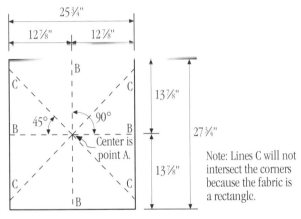

Note: Lines C will not intersect the corners because the fabric is a rectangle.

Step 2. With a fine-point black felt pen, trace the entire design from the pullout pattern onto a 28" x 28" piece of tracing paper. Trace the design in Quadrants 1 and 3 first, pivoting at "A." Then flip the tracing paper onto the backside and trace Quadrants 3 and 4, pivoting at "A."

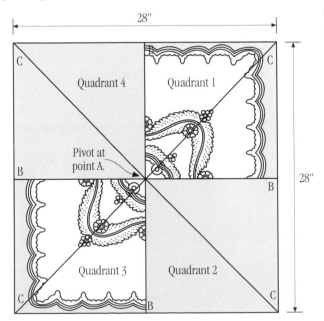

Step 3. Place the tracing-paper pattern under the fabric. Center it by using the quadrant and diagonal lines that are drawn on the fabric rectangle. Pin to avoid movement. Trace the design around the outer edges and the design motifs in the center. Use a sharp, medium-lead pencil.

Step 4. Choose any quadrant of the design. Make a point approximately in the middle of its diagonal line (line C). Using a square ruler for accuracy, trace one line across this quarter of the quilt, perpendicular to the diagonal. Repeat every 3/16" in both directions. Do the same in the remaining 3 quadrants. These lines, when stitched, form the channels through which you will pull the cording. (Refer to the quilt plan on page 38.)

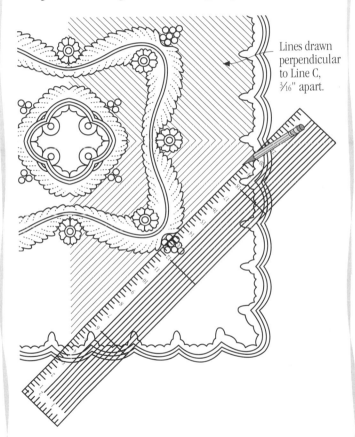

Lines drawn perpendicular to Line C, 3/16" apart.

Stitching

Step 1. Place the prepared rectangle of fabric on top of the remaining fabric rectangle. Smooth out any wrinkles. Align the raw edges and baste together with long stitches. Place your work loosely in the quilting hoop.

Step 2. Starting in the center, sew the two layers together with small running stitches. Complete all the design motifs around the outer edge and in the center before starting to stitch the diagonal lines. (As in quilting, hide the thread knot between the two layers of fabric.) Take the work out of the hoop.

Boutis Provençal

☙ Stuffing

To do boutis, you must create an opening in one layer of fabric so you can stuff the designs with the narrow batting strips. To do this, you use an orange stick to separate the threads. (See page 85.) *Do not* cut the fabric. The process takes some time, so be patient. Do not overstuff or understuff; the quilt should remain supple. Close the openings by moving the threads back into place with the orange stick or a pin. Finish the stuffing before you begin cording.

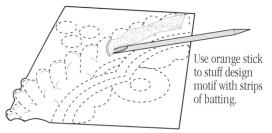

Use orange stick to stuff design motif with strips of batting.

CORDING

Step 1. Thread trapunto or tapestry needle with a 12"–15" length of cotton yarn. Depending on the thickness of the yarn, you will use 2 strands in the narrow channels and 3 or 4 in the others. *Do not* knot the yarn.

Step 2. Working on the back side, insert the needle between threads of the fabric as you did when stuffing. Gently pull the cotton yarn through each stitched channel.

Step 3. Exit the needle on the same side of the work as you entered. Clip the yarn close to the needle exit point and use the tip of the needle to poke the end of the yarn into the hole. Close the opening as you did when you completed the stuffing.

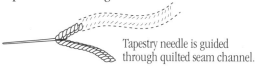

Tapestry needle is guided through quilted seam channel.

TIP   When cording designs that have sharp corners or tight curves, bring the needle with the yarn out of the channel on the back side of the quilt top. Reinsert the needle in the same hole and pull the yarn through the channel carefully.
Be sure not to leave a loop of cording outside the channel. Also, do not pull the yarn completely out of the channel.

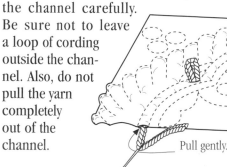

Pull gently.

Boutis Provençal

☙ Finishing

Step 1. Trim the edges of the two layers, following the curves of the scalloped border so that a ¼"-wide seam allowance remains. Bind with a narrow bias binding made from the white fabric, following the curved edge.

Step 2. Wash your finished boutis in cold water with a neutral, pH-balanced soap, such as Ivory®. Rinse well, roll in a towel, and squeeze out excess moisture. Dry flat. Never iron. Due to the shrinkage, any gaps caused by the orange stick or needle will become invisible. The uncut cotton threads will tighten, and the work will be almost identical on both sides, thus reversible.

Boutis items made by Renée Gosse.

Learn More About the Boutis Provençal

The boutis is ancient, but our first knowledge of it in Europe dates from the thirteenth century in Sicily. In the southern part of France (Provence), the technique appeared in the sixteenth century, but it became widespread in the seventeenth century during the reign of Louis XIV. The name boutis comes from a provençal word meaning 'bourrer' or 'to stuff'. The name was also used for the tool used to stuff—a long, flexible needle. Provençal women made wedding petticoats, baby bonnets, bibs, and counterpanes with elaborate hand stitching. With the advent of the sewing machine, delicate handwork became less and less prevalent, and the boutis was almost completely forgotten. There is now a resurgence of interest, and once again, French women are producing these works of art.

Country French
(Campagne Française)

For a young French girl who loved sewing and wanted to learn English, it was a dream come true to work in a San Francisco quilt shop. That was fifteen years ago— my first visit to the United States and my first exposure to quilts. My star (Le Moyne? Feathered? Ohio?) was surely guiding me. I fell in love with quilts immediately and knew my destiny lay in that direction. I particularly loved the bi-colored quilts and, most of all, the ones that were red and white.

A few years ago, when Diane de Obaldia asked me to design a country-style quilt to be sold as a kit at Le Rouvray, I chose red and white as a basis. In France, quilters were not yet into mixing many different geometric patterns. However, we had a great collection of them at Le Rouvray and I liked the idea. I had already mixed various shades of red when I discovered that the addition of red-orange fabrics brought light and warmth to the palette. The kit is still one of our best sellers. We have seen our clients make this pattern in many variations of colors, and it works every time!

Cosabeth Parriaud

Country French, by Cosabeth Parriaud, 1991, Paris, France, 56⅛" x 56⅛". Machine pieced and hand quilted.

🐚 Quilt size: 56⅛" x 56⅛"

Finished block size: 6⅜" x 6⅜"

French Country Block
Finished size:
6⅜" x 6⅜"
Make 36.

🐚 Materials: 44"-wide fabric

¼ yd. each of 7 different red, red-orange, and bur-
    gundy printed fabrics (stripes, plaids, polka dots,
    checks) for block centers
1¾ yds. off-white for background
1¾ yds. burgundy checked fabric for sashing and
    border
½ yd. of dark burgundy print for cornerstones in the
    sashing and border
3½ yds. for backing
¼ yd. dark red solid for binding

🐚 Cutting

Instructions that follow are for rotary cutting. If you
choose to draft your own templates, make them as
shown. The measurements include ¼"-wide seam
allowances.

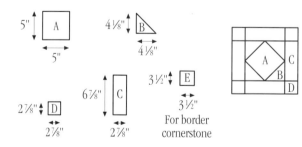

From the 7 **red, red-orange,** and **burgundy** printed
fabrics, cut 36 squares, each 5" x 5". (Cut 5 each from
6 fabrics and 6 from 1 fabric.) For added variety, cut a
few of the squares slightly off-grain. (Or cut 36
Template A.)

From the **off-white** fabric, cut 8 strips, each 4⅛" x
42"; crosscut into 72 squares, each 4⅛" x 4⅛". Cut
each square once diagonally to yield 144 triangles for
background. (Or cut 144 Template B.)

From the **burgundy checked** fabric, cut:

   4 strips lengthwise, each 3½" x 52", for borders
   8 strips lengthwise, each 2⅞" x 60"; crosscut into
     60 rectangles, each 2⅞" x 6⅞", for sashing strips
     (or cut 60 Template C)

From the **dark burgundy** print, cut:

   2 strips, each 2⅞" x 42"; crosscut into 25 squares,
     each 2⅞" x 2⅞", for sashing cornerstones (or
     cut 25 Template D)
   4 squares, each 3½" x 3½", for border corner-
     stones (or cut 4 Template E)

🐚 Assembling the Blocks and Quilt Top

Use accurate ¼"-wide seam allowances.

Step 1. Piece each block as shown. Trim or square up
each block if necessary. Make 36 blocks.

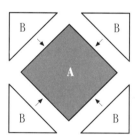

Step 2. Piece together vertical rows of 6 blocks with
sashing strips between each block. Arrange the blocks
in random order. Make 6 rows.

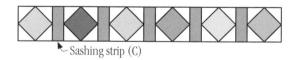

Sashing strip (C)

Step 3. Piece sashing strips with 2⅞" x 2⅞" sashing
cornerstones as shown. Make 5.

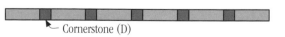

Cornerstone (D)

Step 4. Join the vertical rows, making sure to match the seams between the blocks, sashing, and sashing cornerstones.

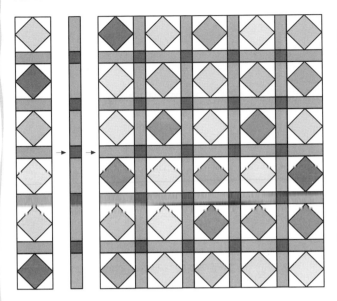

Step 5. Add the side borders. Measure and cut as directed for borders with straight-cut corners on page 87.

Step 6. Add the top and bottom borders, measuring the width of the quilt top only. Do not include the side borders. Trim the 2 remaining border strips to that measurement and stitch the 3½" dark burgundy cornerstones to the ends of the strips. Sew them to the top and bottom edges of the quilt top. Press.

Finishing the Quilt

Step 1. Layer the quilt top with batting and backing; baste.

Step 2. Quilt as desired or follow quilting suggestion.

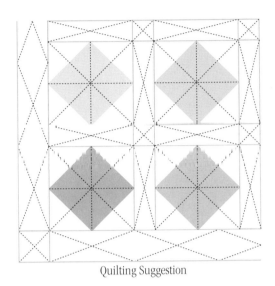

Quilting Suggestion

Step 3. Bind edges with 1¼"-wide straight-grain strips of the dark red solid fabric. (See page 92.)

Country French

Rétais Bows
(Noeuds papillons réthais)

The inhabitants of the Île de Ré are known as Rétais. I am of French Huguenot descent, and my family is from this island, which seems to float somewhere between the blue of the Atlantic and the blue of the sky, just across the bridge from La Rochelle, a place that was important in French Protestant history.

Every summer, I visit my relatives, who still live on the island. The climate is mild and flowers grow everywhere. As early as February, flowers spill over the tops of walls and out of every corner. In summer, thousands of hollyhocks line the narrow streets and bloom in every garden. In the small courtyards that are typical here, geraniums flourish year 'round. The small blue-and-white houses with blue-green shutters have a happy and peaceful look. Even if I only go there for a few days, I feel mentally and physically rested.

I wanted to capture the blues of the island and decided to make a small quilt using my favorite pattern, the Bow Tie. When my friends and clients at Le Rouvray heard about my project, they began giving me scraps of blue. Then I started piecing... and piecing... and piecing! The blues kept arriving. When I had 225 bows made from 225 different fabrics, I decided it was time to stop and put the quilt together. I naturally baptized the quilt "Rétais Bows."

Viviane
Martin-Schloesing

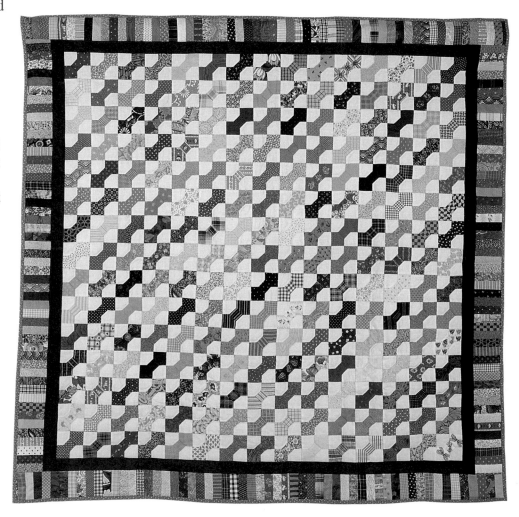

Rétais Bows, by Viviane Martin-Schloesing, 1993, Grigny, France, 50" x 50". Hand pieced and hand quilted.

44

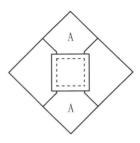

❧ Quilt size: 50" x 50"

Finished block size: 3" x 3"

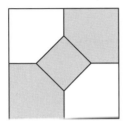

Bow Block
Finished size: 3" x 3"
Make 225.

❧ Materials: 44"-wide fabric

2½ yds. assorted blue prints for bows and outer
    border
1½ yds. off-white for backgrounds
¼ yd. dark blue for inner border
3 yds. blue print for backing and binding

❧ Cutting

Templates are on page 47.

From the assorted **blue** prints, cut:

    450 Template A for bows

    225 squares, each 1⅝" x 1⅝" (Template B), for knots

    See page 46, step 5, for cutting outer border.

From the **off-white** fabric, cut:

    450 Template A for backgrounds

From the **dark blue** fabric, cut:

    5 strips, each 2" x 42", for inner border

❧ Making the Blocks

Use accurate ¼"-wide seam allowances.

Step 1. Stitch 2 bows (Template A) to opposite sides of
1 knot (Template B). Start and stop the stitching ¼"
from the edges of the square. Press seams toward the
bows.

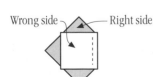

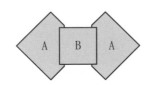

Step 2. Stitch 2 background
pieces (Template A) to the 2
remaining sides of the knot.
Place the background piece
on top of the bow and knot
section, centering it with right
sides together. Turn the unit
over and stitch between the
previously stitched seams.

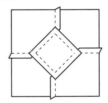

Step 3. Finally, stitch the 4 remaining seams. Match the
outside edges and pin. Turn the seam that connects the
bow to the knot so that you can see where your earlier
stitching line ends. Start stitching at that point, sewing
from the knot toward the outside edge of the block.
Press seams toward the bows.

Step 4. Repeat steps 1–3 to make a total of 225 Bow
Tie blocks.

❧ Assembling the Quilt Top

Step 1. Arrange the blocks in an order that pleases you
in 15 rows of 15 blocks each, referring to the quilt plan
on page 47.

Step 2. Sew the blocks together in groups of 9 blocks
(3 rows of 3 blocks each). You will have 25 group units.

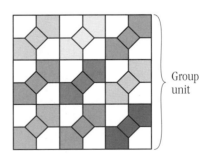

Group
unit

Make 25 group units.

Step 3. Sew the group units together in 5 rows of 5 group units each.

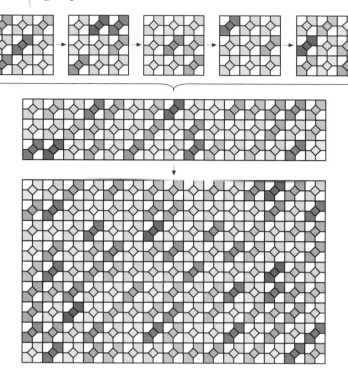

Step 4. Add the inner border, measuring and cutting as directed for borders with straight-cut corners on page 87. Piece the dark blue inner border strips together end-to-end as necessary to equal the measurement of the quilt top. Sew the pieced strips to the top and bottom edges of the quilt top. Measure the length of the quilt, including the top and bottom borders. Cut and piece strips to equal the measurement. Sew the pieced strips to the sides of the quilt top.

Step 5. From the assorted **blue** prints, cut a total of 18 strips, each 1½" x 42" (or see * at right) for outer border. Arrange the strips in random order and sew the long sides together to make 1 strip set. Press all seams in one direction.

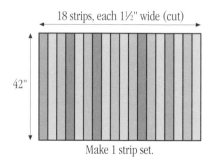

18 strips, each 1½" wide (cut)

42"

Make 1 strip set.

Step 6. Cut 12 strip units, each 3½" wide, from the strip set.

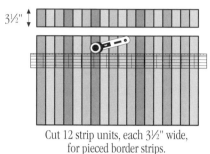

3½"

Cut 12 strip units, each 3½" wide, for pieced border strips.

Step 7. Measure the length of the quilt top. Piece together, end-to-end, lengths of the pieced border strips to equal the measurement. Sew the strips to the sides of the quilt top.

Step 8. Measure the width of the quilt top, including the side borders. Piece together lengths as you did before to equal the measurement. Sew the strips to the top and bottom edges of the quilt top.

*You may cut 198 pieces using Template C and piece the rectangles together to complete the outer borders. Measure the quilt top. Piece rectangles to make border strips to match the measurements. Add the side borders first, then the top and bottom borders.

Finishing the Quilt

Step 1. Layer the quilt top with batting and backing; baste.

Step 2. Quilt as desired or follow quilting suggestion.

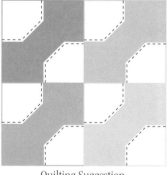

Quilting Suggestion

Step 3. Bind edges with 1¼"-wide straight-grain strips of the blue backing and binding fabric. (See page 92.)

Rétais Bows

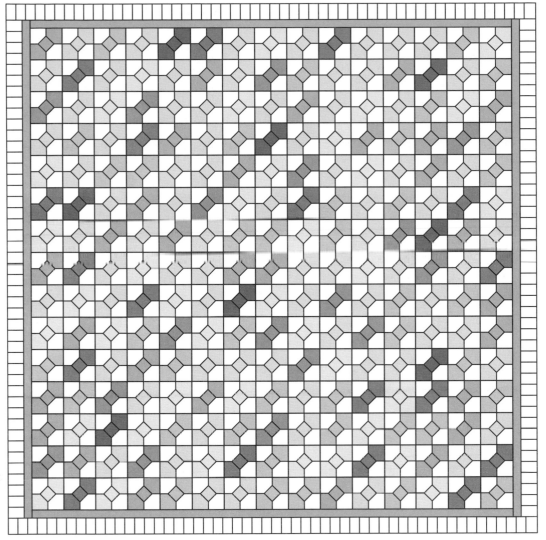

Quilt Plan

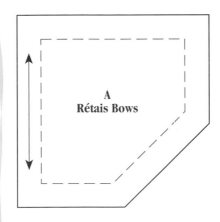

A
Rétais Bows

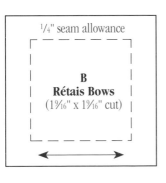

¹/₄" seam allowance

B
Rétais Bows
(1⁹⁄₁₆" x 1⁹⁄₁₆" cut)

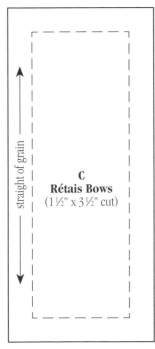

straight of grain

C
Rétais Bows
(1½" x 3½" cut)

Rétais Bows

Autumn Trees in the Luxembourg Gardens

(Les arbres du Luxembourg en Automne)

The chestnut trees in the Luxembourg Gardens in Paris inspired me to make this quilt. I live only minutes away from the gardens, and every day—even in winter—I ride my bicycle alongside the gardens on my way to work at Le Rouvray.

Autumn Trees in the Luxembourg Gardens, by Jacqueline Billion, 1988, Paris, France, 99" x 99". Hand pieced by Jacqueline and hand quilted by a church group in the Philippines.

I find autumn to be the prettiest season in Paris. Many flowers are still in full bloom, yet the chestnut trees start turning a lovely rust color in early September.

Fifty acres of gardens surround the Palace of Luxembourg (now the French Senate), which was built in 1615 during the reign of Marie de Médicis. Many people over the centuries have enjoyed the English-style and French classical gardens, terraces, fountains, ponds, and sculptures. It is a gathering place for nearby Latin Quarter students and also for children who enjoy the puppet shows, pony rides, and the merry-go-round.

South of the main garden lie two smaller, narrower gardens. Each contains six rows of beautiful, old chestnut trees. I have tried to capture the spirit of these trees by using one tree pattern, yet a different shade of rust for each block.

Jacqueline Billion

Jacqueline used the Tree of Life pattern from Pieces of the Past *by Nancy J. Martin.*

Quilt size: 99" x 99"

Finished block size: 12" x 12"

Materials: 44"-wide fabric

25 fat eighths* in different shades of rust (or 3¼ yds.) for Tree blocks

2½ yds. off-white for Tree blocks

3½ yds. pastel print for plain alternating blocks, setting triangles, and middle border

3½ yds. dark floral print for block frames, inner and outer borders, and binding (cut crosswise)**

8¾ yds. for backing

*9" x 22" piece of fabric

**You will need to increase yardage to avoid pieced borders.

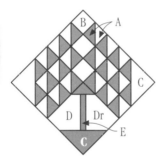

Tree Block
Finished size: 12" x 12"
Make 25.

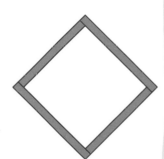

Plain Alternating Block
Make 16.

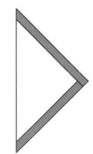

Side Setting Triangles
Make 16.

Corner Setting Triangles
Make 4.

Cutting

Use templates on page 53.

TREE BLOCKS

From each of the 25 **rust** fabrics, cut:

    23 Template A

    1 Template E

    1 Template C

From the **off-white** fabric, cut:

    450 Template A

    75 Template B

    50 Template C

    25 Template D

    25 Template D reversed

From the **pastel** print, cut:

    12 strips, each 1½" x 42", for middle border

    16 squares, each 10½" x 10½", for plain alternating blocks

    4 squares, each 15½" x 15½"; crosscut twice diagonally to yield a total of 16 side setting triangles.

    2 squares, each 7⅞" x 7⅞"; crosscut once diagonally to yield a total of 4 corner setting triangles.

From the **dark floral** print, cut:

    9 strips, each 1½" x 42", for inner border

    10 strips, each 4½" x 42", for outer border

    28 strips, each 1½" x 42"; crosscut into:

    32 strips, each 1½" x 10½", for plain alternating block frames

    32 strips, each 1½" x 12½", for plain alternating block frames

    16 strips, each 1½" x 11½", for side setting triangle frames

    16 strips, each 1½" x 13", for side setting triangle frames

    4 strips, each 1½" x 13", for corner setting triangle frames

    10 strips, each 1¼" x 42", for straight-grain binding

Autumn Trees

 Making the Blocks

Use accurate ¼"-wide seam allowances.

TREE BLOCK

Piece 25 Tree blocks as shown, using a different rust color fabric for each block.

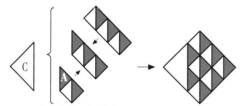

Make 18 for each block.

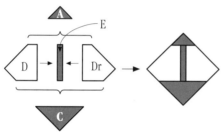

Make 2 for each block.

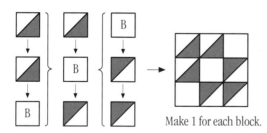

Make 1 for each block.

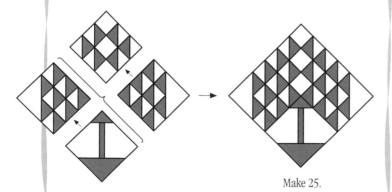

Make 1 for each block.

Make 25.

PLAIN ALTERNATING BLOCKS

Step 1. Sew 1½" x 10½" dark floral print frame strips to 2 opposite sides of a 10½" pastel print square.
Step 2. Sew 1½" x 12½" dark floral print frame strips to the remaining sides.
Step 3. Repeat with the remaining 15 pastel print 10½" squares.

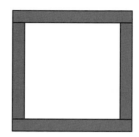

SIDE SETTING TRIANGLES

Step 1. Sew a 1½" x 11½" dark floral print frame strip to a short side of a side setting triangle.
Step 2. Sew a 1½" x 13" frame strip to the other short dark floral print side. Do not trim the excess fabric yet.
Step 3. Repeat with the remaining 15 side setting triangles.

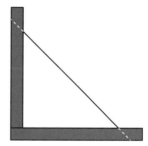

CORNER SETTING TRIANGLES

Step 1. Sew a 1½" x 13" dark floral print frame strip to the long side of a corner setting triangle. Do not trim the excess fabric yet.
Step 2. Repeat with the remaining 3 corner setting triangles.

Autumn Trees

✿ Assembling the Quilt Top

Step 1. Referring to the quilt plan, arrange the blocks with the side and corner setting triangles in diagonal rows. (See "Diagonally Set Quilts" on page 86.) Join the blocks in each row. Press the seams in opposite directions from row to row.

Step 2. Join the rows, making sure to match the seams between blocks. Trim and square up the outside edges after the rows are sewn.

✿ Borders

Borders for this quilt will be joined to the quilt top in a counterclockwise direction, beginning with the right side border. Refer to the quilt plan on page 52.

Step 1. Join the short ends of the inner border strips to make one continuous strip. Do the same with the middle border strips, then the outer border strips.

Join short ends of border strips.

Step 2. Measure the length of the quilt top as directed on page 87, then add 7½" (the width of the combined inner, middle, and outer borders, less seams). Cut pieces from the inner, middle, and outer border strips to this measurement.

Step 3. Stitch the inner, middle, and outer border strips together to make the *right side* border unit. Press seams toward the dark floral strips.

| Inner Border |
| Middle Border |
| Outer Border |

Border Units

Step 4. With pins, mark the center and quarter folds of the right edge of the quilt top. Mark the center and quarter folds of the border unit on the inner border

strip. Your pins should be placed as shown. One pin will be approximately 7½" from the bottom end, and the opposite pin should be on the top edge of the border unit.

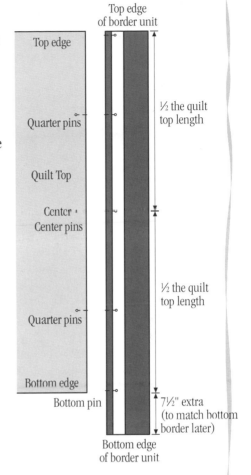

Top edge of border unit

Top edge

Quarter pins

Quilt Top

Center
Center pins

Quarter pins

Bottom edge

Bottom pin

½ the quilt top length

½ the quilt top length

7½" extra (to match bottom border later)

Bottom edge of border unit

Step 5. Pin the border unit to the quilt top, matching center and quarter pins, as well as the top edge of the quilt top with the top edge of the border unit. Match the bottom pin of the border unit with the bottom edge of the quilt top. The bottom end of the border unit will extend beyond the bottom edge of the quilt top.

Step 6. Begin stitching the border unit to the quilt top ¼" in from the top edge of the border unit and stop stitching 12" from the bottom edge. Press seam toward the inner border strip.

Step 7. Measure the width of the quilt top as directed on page 87, then add 7½" (the combined inner, middle, and outer borders, less seams). Cut pieces from the inner, middle, and outer border strips to this measurement.

Step 8. Stitch the strips together to make the *top* border unit. Press seams toward the dark floral strips.

Step 9. Mark the center and quarter folds of the quilt top and the top border unit. Also mark half the width of the quilt top in each direction from the center pin. Your pins should be placed as shown.

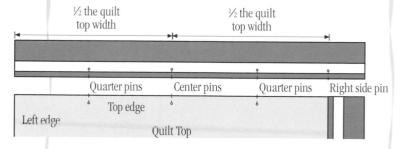

Step 10. Pin the border unit to the top edge of the quilt top, matching center and quarter pins as well as the right side pin with the seam line of the quilt top/right side border. Match the left end of the border unit with the left edge of the quilt top.

Step 11. Begin stitching the border unit to the quilt top ¼" in from one end of the border unit and stop stitching ¼" from the other end. Press seam toward the inner border strip.

Step 12. Measure the length of the quilt top including the top borders. Cut pieces from the inner, middle, and outer border strips to this measurement.

Step 13. Stitch the strips together to make the *left side* border unit. Press seams toward the dark floral strips.

Step 14. Mark the center and quarter folds of the left side of the quilt top and the border unit as you did for the right border. Also mark half the length of the quilt top in each direction from the center pin.

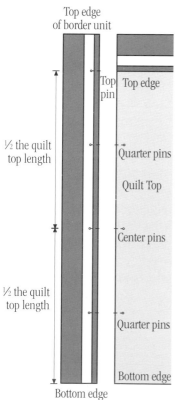

Step 15. Pin the border unit to the quilt top, matching the center and quarter pins as well as the top pin with the seam line of the quilt top/top border. Match the bottom end of the border unit with the bottom edge of the quilt top.

Step 16. Begin stitching the border unit to the quilt top ¼" in from one end of the border unit and stop stitching ¼" from the other end. Press seam toward the inner border strip.

Step 17. Measure the width of the quilt top, including the left side border. Cut pieces from the inner, middle, and outer border strips to this measurement.

Step 18. Stitch the strips together to make the *bottom* border unit. Press seams toward the dark floral strips.

Step 19. Mark the center and quarter folds of the bottom edge of the quilt top and the border unit as you did for the top border. Also mark half the width of the quilt top in each direction from the center pin.

Step 20. Pin the border unit to the quilt top, matching the pins as you did with the previous border. Match the left and right ends of the bottom border unit as shown.

Quilt Plan   Sew last 12" of right border after joining the bottom border to the quilt top.

Step 21. Stitch the border unit to the quilt top. Sew the remaining 12" of the right side border to complete the border.

Finishing the Quilt

Step 1. Layer the quilt top with batting and backing; baste. Quilt as desired.

Step 2. Bind the edges with straight-grain strips of dark floral print fabric. (See page 92.)

Autumn Trees

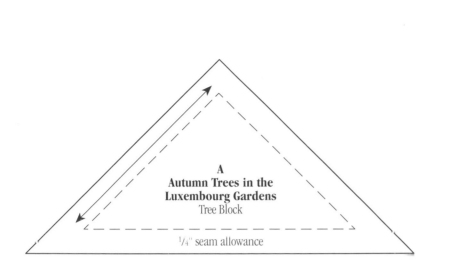

A
**Autumn Trees in the
Luxembourg Gardens**
Tree Block

¹/₄" seam allowance

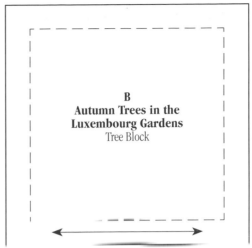

B
**Autumn Trees in the
Luxembourg Gardens**
Tree Block

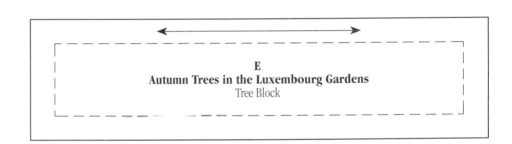

E
Autumn Trees in the Luxembourg Gardens
Tree Block

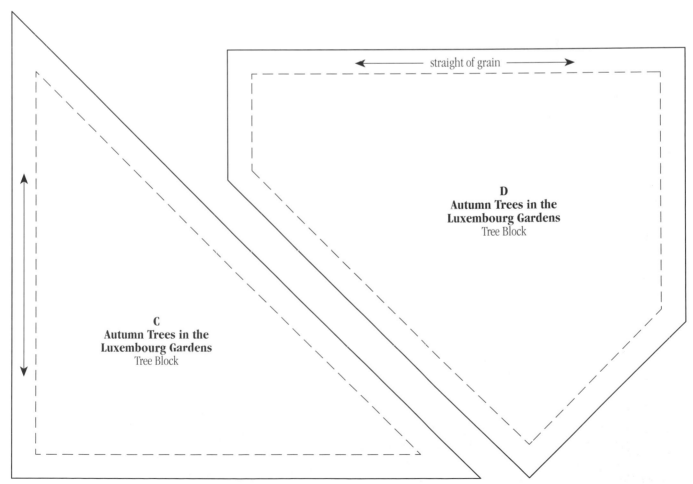

straight of grain

D
**Autumn Trees in the
Luxembourg Gardens**
Tree Block

C
**Autumn Trees in the
Luxembourg Gardens**
Tree Block

Autumn Trees

The Flea Market Pineapple

(L'ananas du Marché aux Puces)

I've always loved flea markets! Long before I began making quilts, I spent my weekends (and my francs) picking up treasures from the bottoms of baskets or boxes at flea markets. I enjoyed dressing in fashions from the 1920s and '30s, because no one else was dressing the same way. I never threw my treasures away.

When the quilt bug bit me (fortunately not a flea), I rummaged through drawers and cupboards and found a red sleeve, a burgundy shirt, and a beautiful red paisley shawl (with a few moth holes I could cut around). So, I decided to make a red quilt, with not just one red, but all shades of red, from the wildest to the dullest tones. I wanted my quilt to palpitate with the color of blood, which is the color of life. I decided to punctuate the reds with black to heighten the dramatic effect. My drawers and closets didn't disappoint me. I assembled a multitude of scraps that did not look spectacular by themselves but, once linked and placed next to one another, took on a new youth that would not be affected by passing years or passing styles. My "Flea Market Pineapple" was born.

Christine Meynier

The Flea Market Pineapple, by Christine Meynier, 1991, Chaville, France, 44" x 44". Machine pieced and hand quilted.

Quilt size: 44" x 44"

Finished block size: 12" x 12"

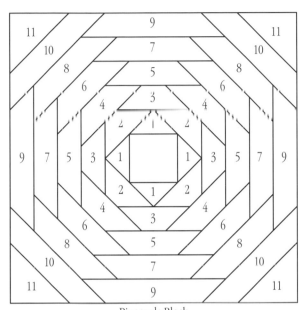

Pineapple Block
Finished Size: 12" x 12"

Materials: 44"-wide fabric

⅛ yd. each of 4 different black prints or solids for logs
(Label Fabrics A, B, C, and D.)

⅛ yd. each of 3 different bright red small-scale prints
for logs (Label Fabrics E, F, and G.)

¼ yd. each of 4 different bright red large-scale prints
for logs (Label Fabrics H, I, J, and K.)

½ yd. each of 2 different muted red paisleys for logs
(Label Fabrics L and M.)

⅓ yd. burgundy print for logs (Label Fabric N.)

½ yd. dark burgundy solid for logs and binding (Label
Fabric O.)

¼ yd. light burgundy solid for logs (Label Fabric P.)

Scraps of brown for chimney of center block (Label
Fabric Q.)

Scraps of yellow for row #1 of center block (Label
Fabric R.)

¼ yd. each of 2 different browns for outer triangles
(Label Fabrics S and T.)

1 yd. black-burgundy-and-gray print or ikat-style fabric
for border

2½ yds. fabric for backing

12 copies of the Pineapple pattern (on page 58) for
foundation piecing (See "Making the Blocks," step
1, on page 56.)

The directions that follow are to make 4 corner
blocks, 4 side blocks, and 1 center block.

Cutting

Refer to the color photo and Fabric and Piecing
plans for each block. Always cut the pieces requiring
templates first, then the fabric strips for the other logs.

For logs #2–10, cut 1½" x 42" strips from the
fabrics indicated on the Piecing and Fabric plans for
each block.

For the chimneys in the center block and the side
blocks, use Template #1; for the chimneys in the corner
blocks, use Template #2; for log #1, use Template #3,
and for log #11, use Template #4. The templates are on
page 58.

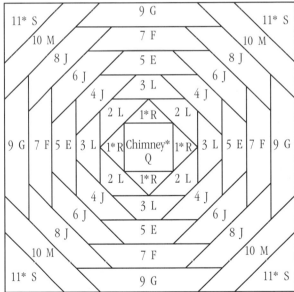

Fabric and Piecing Plan
Center Block
Make 1.
* For chimney, use Template #1.
* For log #1, use Template #3.
* For log #11, use Template #4.

Flea Market Pineapple

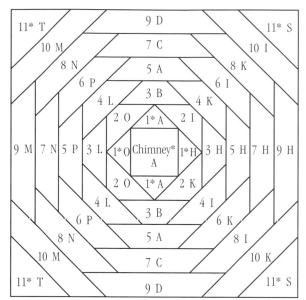

Fabric and Piecing Plan
Side Block
Make 4.
* For chimney, use Template #1.
* For log #1, use Template #3.
* For log #11, use Template #4.

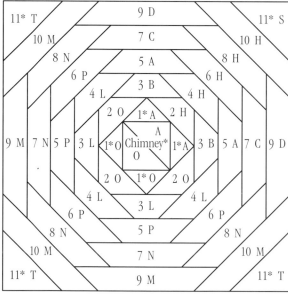

Fabric and Piecing Plan
Corner Block
Make 4.
* For chimney, use Template #2.
* For log #1, use Template #3.
* For log #11, use Template #4.

❧ Making the Blocks

Use accurate ¼"-wide seam allowances. All the marked lines on the paper foundation are the seam lines. All fabric logs are positioned on the *unmarked side* of the paper. Finger-press each log open over the space it is to cover on the paper. Make sure that an adequate seam allowance extends into the adjacent areas. Add each log in a clockwise direction, stitching on the seam line. To reduce bulk, trim seam allowances to ⅛"–³⁄₁₆" wide. Turn the block over, fold the foundation back out of the way, then trim.

Step 1. To prepare the block foundation, photocopy the pattern, enlarging it 200% (doubling the size). Because different copy machines may produce copies with a slight variance, always be sure to make all copies for each project on the same machine, from the original block in this book. Be sure there is a margin of 1" on each side of the block.

Make 12 copies (3 will be for practice, if you like). You will stitch the fabric pieces directly onto the paper copies. After stitching is complete, remove the paper.

Step 2. Follow the piecing sequence in the illustrations above. For the corner blocks, stitch the two chimney triangles (Template #2) together to make the chimney. Place the chimney, right side up, on the unmarked side of the paper. Make sure the edges of the square extend into the adjacent areas. Pin in place. Place the first log #1 on top of the center square, right sides together, along the joining seam line. Pin in place. *Make sure both fabrics extend at least ¼" beyond the seam lines.*

Pieced Chimney for Corner Blocks
Make 4 using Template #2.

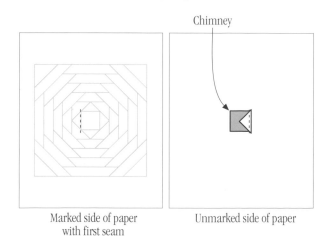

Marked side of paper with first seam   Unmarked side of paper

Flea Market Pineapple

Step 3. Carefully turn the paper over so that the marked side of the paper faces up, holding the log and center square in place. Pin in place. Stitch on the line, through the layers of the paper and the 2 pieces.

Step 4. Finger-press log #1 open over the area it is to cover on the paper foundation. Trim the excess fabric, being careful to leave a seam allowance that extends into the adjacent areas.

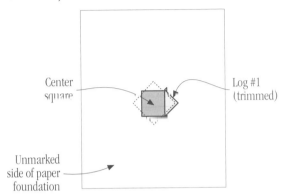

Center square

Log #1 (trimmed)

Unmarked side of paper foundation

Step 5. Working in a clockwise direction, add the next log #1, placing it on the center square, right sides together. Stitch. Finger-press and trim as you did before. Continue adding the logs in numerical order, and in a clockwise direction until the design is complete. Make 4 corner blocks, 4 side blocks, and 1 center block.

Step 6. Press completed blocks and trim to square up the edges, leaving a ¼" seam allowance beyond the outer line of the marked square on the paper foundation.

Assembling the Quilt Top

Step 1. Arrange the blocks as shown in the quilt plan. Refer to the color photo for specific orientation of the blocks and color placement.

Step 2. Sew the blocks together into 3 rows of 3 blocks each. Press the seams between each block.

Step 3. Sew the rows together, making sure to match the seams between each block.

Step 4. Add the borders, measuring and cutting as directed for mitered corners on page 88. From the black-gray-and-burgundy print, cut 5 strips, each 4½" x 42". Stitch border strips together to equal the measurements of the quilt top. Stitch the borders to the sides, then to the top and bottom edges of the quilt top.

Finishing the Quilt

Step 1. Layer the quilt top with batting and backing; baste.

Step 2. Quilt as desired.

Step 3. Bind the edges with 1¼"-wide straight-grain strips of the burgundy solid fabric. (See page 92.)

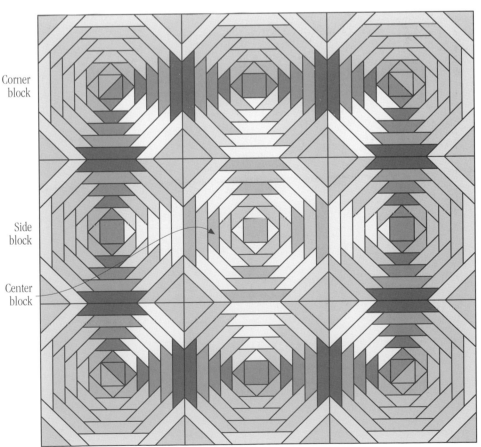

Corner block

Side block

Center block

Quilt Plan

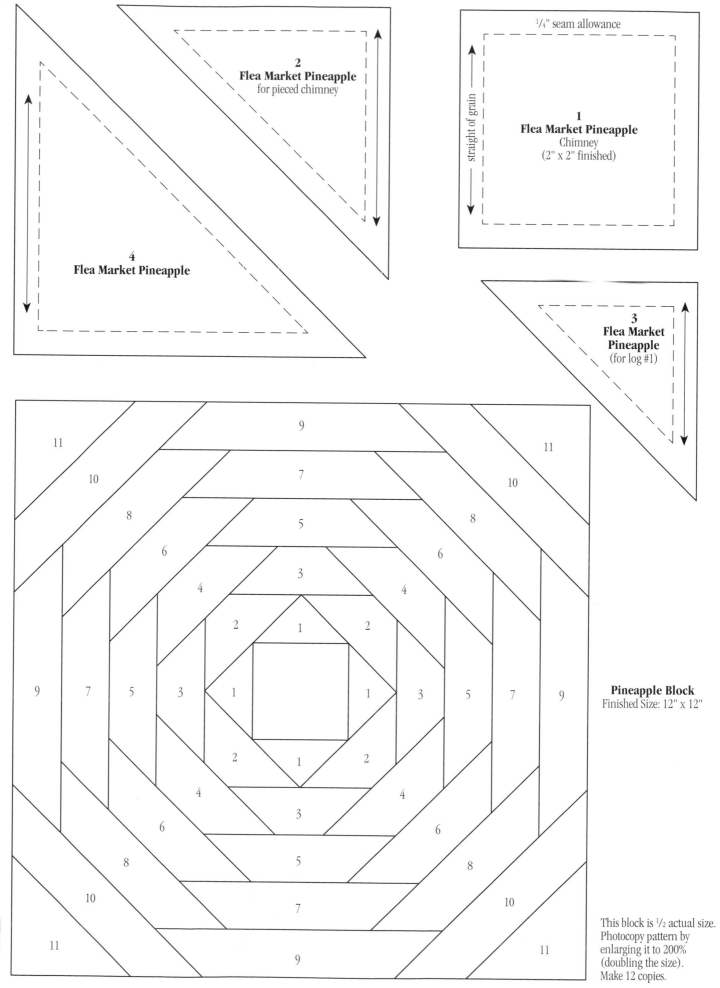

2
Flea Market Pineapple
for pieced chimney

¼" seam allowance

1
Flea Market Pineapple
Chimney
(2" x 2" finished)

straight of grain

4
Flea Market Pineapple

3
Flea Market Pineapple
(for log #1)

9

11   11

10   7   10

8   5   8

6   3   6

4   4

2   1   2

9 7 5 3   1   1   3 5 7 9

Pineapple Block
Finished Size: 12" x 12"

2   1   2

4   4

3

6   6

8   5   8

10   7   10

11   11

9

This block is ½ actual size.
Photocopy pattern by
enlarging it to 200%
(doubling the size).
Make 12 copies.

The Squares of Montmartre (Les squares de Montmartre)

Today Joëlle de Bailliencourt and I work together at Le Rouvray. We met fifteen years ago when we were "square mothers" in Montmartre. That means, that like many city mothers, we chose the nearest playground, and while the children played, we sat on benches—on sunny and stormy days.

In Paris, these playgrounds are often in neighborhood squares. The square is usually surrounded by an iron fence and in the center there is a statue of an artist or statesman. The statue's head serves as a perch for the local pigeons!

The first time I saw Joëlle, she was appliquéing a small brown bear on a baby quilt and I was sewing a quilt top.

We knew then that we were destined to be friends—and we have been ever since. Joëlle plans her quilts, but I am an instinctive quilter. My quilts "happen." The "Squares of Montmartre" is no exception. It started with a few Ninepatch squares made on a rainy winter day. Later, I was browsing in my beloved Montmartre and found a lovely red-and-blue checked pillowcase at a junk sale. After that I found a pink fabric that matched the blocks perfectly. I have made six Ninepatch quilts and this one is my favorite.

Joëlle no longer lives in Montmartre, but she remembers with nostalgia the steps, the squares, and the winding streets. She visits me often and we usually go to see my husband, who is one of the painters setting up their easels every day on the famous Place du Tertre. Montmartre is a lucky place for painters and quilters alike.

Willemke Vidinic

The Squares of Montmartre, by Willemke Vidinic, 1991, Paris, France, 73¾" x 73¾". Hand pieced and hand quilted.

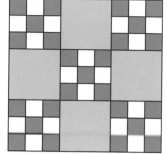

✿ Quilt size: 73¾" x 73¾"

FINISHED BLOCK SIZES:

Single Ninepatch Block
Finished size: 3" x 3"
Make 108.

Double Ninepatch Block
(Use 5 Ninepatch blocks in each)
Finished size: 9" x 9"
Make 16.

✿ Materials: 44"-wide fabric

1½ yds. assorted blue prints (or scraps) for Single Ninepatch blocks

1 yd. off-white for Single Ninepatch blocks

1 yd. blue-and-pink plaid fabric for Double Ninepatch blocks and second border

3½ yds. pink fabric for setting blocks and triangles, and second and fourth borders

¼ yd. navy blue checked fabric for corner squares in the second and fourth borders

½ yd. blue-and-white checked fabric for first and third borders

4½ yds. for backing*

*This yardage allows for a backing that wraps to finish the edge as a self-binding, so make sure your backing fabric coordinates with the the quilt design and the other fabrics in the quilt top.

✿ Cutting

Instructions that follow are for rotary cutting. If you choose to draft your own templates for the blocks and pieced second border, make them as shown. The measurements include ¼"-wide seam allowances.

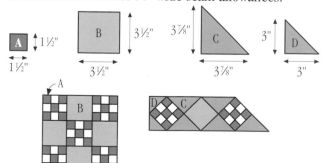

From the assorted **blue** prints, cut 540 squares, each 1½" x 1½", for pieced blocks (or cut 540 Template A).

From the **off-white** fabric, cut 16 strips, each 1½" x 42"; crosscut into 432 squares, each 1½" x 1½", for pieced blocks (or cut 432 Template A).

From the **blue** and **pink plaid**, cut 8 strips, each 3½" x 42"; crosscut into 88 squares, each 3½" x 3½", for Double Ninepatch blocks and second border (or cut 88 Template B).

From the **pink** fabric, cut:

4 strips, each 5½" x 64½", for fourth border

9 squares, each 9½" x 9½", for plain alternating blocks

3 squares, each 14" x 14"; cut twice diagonally to yield 12 triangles for side setting triangles

2 squares, each 7¼" x 7¼"; cut once diagonally to yield 4 triangles for corner setting triangles

4 strips, each 5½" x 42"; crosscut into 24 squares, each 5½" x 5½". Cut each square twice diagonally to yield 96 triangles for second border side setting triangles (or cut 96 Template C).

8 squares, each 3" x 3"; cut once diagonally to yield 16 triangles for second border corner setting triangles (or cut 16 Template D).

From the **navy blue checked** fabric, cut:

4 squares, each 4¾" x 4¾, for second border corner squares

4 squares, each 5½" x 5½", for fourth border corner squares

From the **blue-and-white checked** fabric, cut 16 strips, each 1" x 42", for the first and third borders.

✿ Making the Blocks

SINGLE NINEPATCH BLOCKS

Piece together 4 off-white and 5 blue 1½" squares as shown. Make 108 blocks.

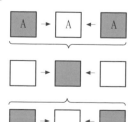

Squares of Montmartre

DOUBLE NINEPATCH BLOCKS

Piece together 5 Single Ninepatch blocks and 4 blue-and-pink plaid 3½" squares as shown. Make 16 blocks.

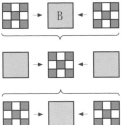

⚜ Assembling the Quilt Top

Step 1. Referring to the quilt plan, arrange the Double Ninepatch and pink plain alternating blocks in diagonal rows, with the pink side and corner setting triangles. (See "Diagonally Set Quilts" on page 86.) Join the blocks in each row. Press the seams in opposite directions from row to row.

Step 2. Join the rows, making sure to match the seams between blocks. Trim and square up the outside edges after the rows are sewn if needed.

Step 3. Add the blue-and-white checked first border, measuring and cutting as directed for borders with straight-cut corners on page 87. Piece border strips together as necessary to equal the measurements of the quilt top.

Step 4. Make the second border by piecing Single Ninepatch blocks, blue-and-pink plaid 3½" squares, and pink second border side and corner setting triangles as shown. Make 4.

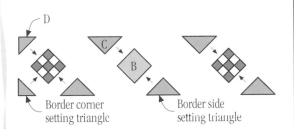

Border corner setting triangle

Border side setting triangle

Make 4.

Step 5. Sew the pieced second border to the quilt top, adding the 4¾" navy blue checked corner squares. (See "Borders with Corner Squares" on pages 87–88.)

Step 6. Add the blue-and-white checked third border as you did for the first border.

Step 7. Sew the pink fourth border to the quilt top, adding the 5½" navy blue checked corner squares as you did for the second border.

⚜ Finishing the Quilt

Step 1. Make the backing. Make sure it extends 3" beyond all edges of the quilt top.

Step 2. Layer the quilt top with batting and backing; baste.

Step 3. Quilt as desired.

Step 4. Follow the directions on page 93–94 for self-binding (finishing the quilt with the backing). The finished "binding" width is ½" on the front of the quilt.

Squares of Montmartre

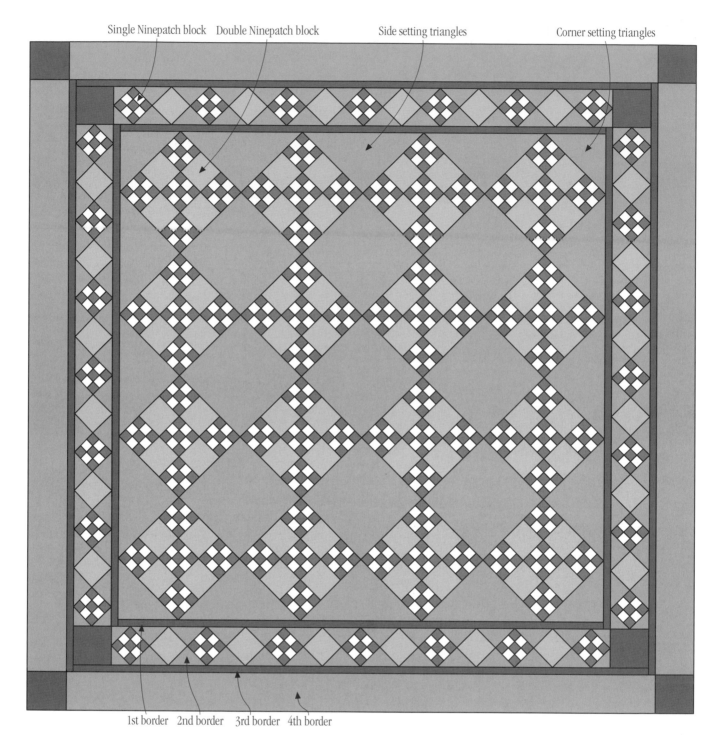

Single Ninepatch block Double Ninepatch block Side setting triangles Corner setting triangles

1st border 2nd border 3rd border 4th border

Quilt Plan

Squares of Montmartre

Afro-Canadian Maple Leaves
(Feuilles d'érables afro-canadiennes)

Senegal is one of the African countries that became a French colony in the nineteenth century. My great-grandfather was the first of my family to leave France and make his life there. My grandparents, parents, and I were all born in Senegal; I spent the first seventeen years of my life in that unforgetable atmosphere of warmth and gaiety.

The African fabrics that surrounded and fascinated me from my earliest childhood were the *pagnes* (French term for loincloth or sarong). The designs are waxed onto the cloth. A pagne wrapped around the head is a kerchief; wrapped around a baby, it's a baby carrier; and around the body, it's a sarong or loincloth. Several sewn together make a *boubou* (African dress). Knot one and it becomes a shopping bag. Of course, they can also be spread out for use as a tablecloth or bedcover.

At home in Paris, I still decorate with these versatile fabrics and I wouldn't think of traveling without one or several! After completing a sewing project, I have always saved pieces of these African fabrics for "something." One day, I started assembling squares and triangles. A Canadian friend was enthusiastic and complimented me on my "patchwork" (a new word for me). Because it was the beginning of my passion for patchwork and quilting along with the beginning of a beautiful friendship, I decided to honor both events by making a quilt with the Maple Leaf pattern, the national emblem of Canada. The fabrics are from the collection of indigo pagnes I brought from Africa.

Joëlle de Bailliencourt

Afro-Canadian Maple Leaves, by Joëlle de Bailliencourt, Paris, France, 81" x 96". Machine pieced in 1989 and hand quilted in 1993.

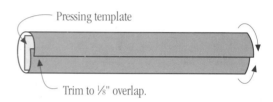

❧ Quilt size: 81" x 96"

Finished block size: 7½" x 7½"

❧ Materials: 44"-wide fabric

5½ yds. assorted blue fabrics*
4 yds. off-white prints
6 yds. for backing**

*Joëlle used 120 different scraps, each 7" x 10".
**This yardage allows for a backing that wraps to finish the edge as a self-binding, so make sure your backing fabric coordinates with the quilt design and the other fabrics in the quilt top.

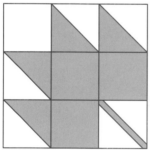

Maple Leaf Block
Finished size: 7½" x 7½"
Make 120.

❧ Cutting

The directions that follow are for rotary cutting. For template cutting, use the templates on page 65. If you are using a number of different fabrics, organize them by block, so that you do not mix up the pieces.

Cutting directions are for 1 block
(For quilt shown, make 120 blocks.)

From the **blue** fabrics, cut:

    3 squares, each 3" x 3" (or cut 3 Template A)

    2 squares, each 3⅜" x 3⅜"; crosscut once diago-nally to yield 4 triangles (or cut 4 Template B)

    1 rectangle, ¾" x 4" (or cut 1 Template C)

From the **off-white** fabric, cut:

    2 squares, each 3" x 3" (or cut 2 Template A)

    2 squares, each 3⅜" x 3⅜"; crosscut once diago nally to yield 4 triangles (or cut 4 Template B)

❧ Making the Blocks

Use accurate ¼"-wide seam allowances, except as noted for appliquéing the leaf stems.

Step 1. To prepare the stem square, cut a ⅜" x 4" rectangle from card stock; a file folder works well. This will be your pressing template. Place a ¾" x 4" blue rectangle, wrong side up, on your ironing board. Placc the pressing-template rectangle in the center of the fabric rectangle. Press one long side of the fabric over the template so that a little more than ⅛" of the fabric overlaps one side of the template. Fold the second side over the template and press. Trim so that there is a ⅛" overlap. Remove pressing template. Make 1 stem for each Maple Leaf block.

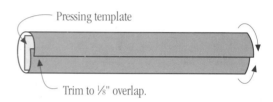

Pressing template

Trim to ⅛" overlap.

Step 2. On an off-white 3" square, draw a diagonal line from corner to corner. Place the stem on the square, folding open the stem as shown, wrong side up. Align the edge of the stem with the diagonal line. Stitch the stem to the square on the pressed fold line.

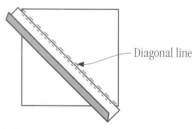

Diagonal line

Step 3. Fold the stem over the seam and hand appliqué the remaining edge, stitching on the folded edge. Trim excess stem around the edges of the square.

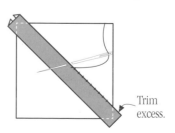

Trim excess.

Step 4. Piece the blocks as shown.

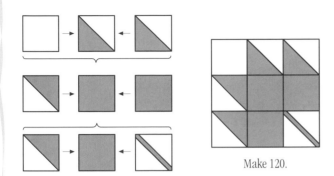

Make 120.

☙ Assembling the Quilt Top

Step 1. Arrange the leaf blocks in units of 4 blocks each, noting the orientation of the leaf stems within each group. Sew the blocks together.

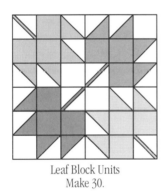

Leaf Block Units
Make 30.

Step 2. Arrange the leaf-block units into 6 rows of 5 block units each. Note the orientation of the units by referring to the photograph on page 63. Sew the blocks together into rows. Press the seams in opposite directions from row to row.

Step 3. Join the rows, making sure to match the seams between the blocks.

☙ Finishing the Quilt

Step 1. Make the backing. Make sure it extends 5" beyond all edges of the quilt top.

Step 2. Layer the quilt top with batting and backing; baste.

Step 3. Quilt as desired.

Step 4. Follow the directions on pages 93–94 for self-binding (finishing the quilt with the backing). The finished "binding" width is 2½" on the quilt front.

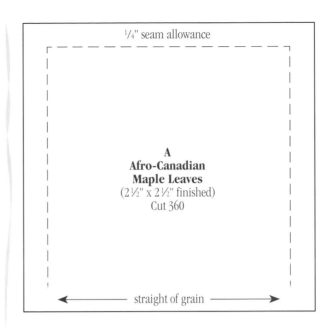

¼" seam allowance

A
**Afro-Canadian
Maple Leaves**
(2½" x 2½" finished)
Cut 360

← straight of grain →

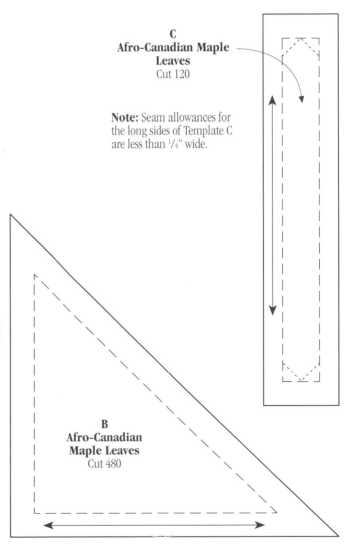

C
**Afro-Canadian Maple
Leaves**
Cut 120

Note: Seam allowances for the long sides of Template C are less than ¼" wide.

B
**Afro-Canadian
Maple Leaves**
Cut 480

Afro-Canadian Maple Leaves

Flowers of Brittany

(Fleurs de Bretagne)

Brittany is a wonderful place for a child to grow up. I am lucky to have had that experience, as I was born and raised in Carnac, one of the most visited places in Brittany.

Beautiful sand beaches, the sea air, a mild climate, and the world-renowned megaliths attract visitors from all over France as well as from elsewhere. The menhirs and dolmens are the megalithic stones that were placed there centuries ago, for still unknown and mysterious reasons.

My grandfather's farm was not far from the city. I used to picnic and dream among the wild flowers and megaliths in a nearby field. My interest in the wild flowers of Brittany surely began there.

This quilt is one of my favorites because it represents those flowers, and I wanted to make an album of the flowers that are typical of the region. There is only one exception— the Anthurium (Block #7). I was pleased to introduce this intended error that follows the tradition of antique quilts. I designed each flower myself, as I do for all my appliqué quilts. It took me eighteen months to complete the quilt, including two hundred hours for the border alone! This quilt was made for a contest, the theme of which was "Regions of France," and it received a special mention from the jury.

Annick Huet

Annick used traditional, needle-turn, and raised-appliqué techniques along with trapunto and cording to complete this striking quilt.

Flowers of Brittany, by Annick Huet, 1992, Paris, France, 59" x 59". Hand appliquéd and hand quilted. Close-up (above) of rickrack flower.

Quilt size: 59" x 59"

Finished block size: 6½" x 6½"
(Block plans—small illustrations of each on page 70.)

Materials: 44"-wide fabric

3½ yds. white for appliqué
2 yds. white muslin or batiste for border and trapunto lining
3½ yds. white for backing
Assorted scraps of prints and solids in reds, blues, yellows, and greens for appliqué
Approx. 60" x 63" piece of synthetic batting for stuffing the trapunto motifs (or use your leftover scraps of batting)
110 yds. of cotton yarn for cording
Tapestry needle
Trapunto needle
Small embroidery hoop

Cutting

From the **white** fabric, cut:

4 strips, each 7" x 65", for borders

41 squares, each 7" x 7"

4 squares, each 10½" x 10½"; cut twice diagonally to yield 16 side setting triangles

2 squares, each 5½" x 5½"; cut once diagonally to yield 4 corner setting triangles

From the **muslin** or **batiste** for trapunto lining, cut:

4 strips, each 7" x 65", for border

16 squares, each 7" x 7"

4 squares, each 10½" x 10½"; cut twice diagonally to yield 16 side setting triangles

2 squares, each 5½" x 5½"; cut once diagonally to yield 4 corner setting triangles

Making the Blocks

Use patterns on pages 96–99 and on the pullout pattern insert. The trapunto blocks use the same patterns as the appliqué blocks. Each pattern is numbered and labeled for appliqué (A) and trapunto (T). The quilt plan on page 69 indicates the pattern number for each block as well as whether the block is appliqué or trapunto. For example: T 14 is a trapunto

block made with appliqué pattern #14. For the triangles, use trapunto patterns T 26, T 27, T 28, T 29, and T 30.

Suggested appliqué techniques are indicated with each pattern.

APPLIQUÉ

Make 25 appliqué blocks. Appliqué techniques begin on page 80. For the Camelia block, Annick made a braided rickrack flower. The directions for making it are on page 84. Select your own color scheme or refer to the photo on page 66 for color placement of the appliqué pieces.

TRAPUNTO

Step 1. Make the trapunto blocks—16 squares, 16 large triangles, and 4 small corner triangles. Refer to the trapunto techniques on page 85.
Step 2. Trapunto the 4 border strips in the same manner as the blocks. Note that the border has mitered corners.

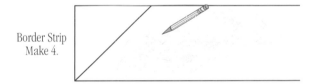

Border Strip
Make 4.

Assembling the Quilt Top

Use accurate ¼"-wide seam allowances.

Step 1. Referring to the quilt plan on page 69, arrange the appliqué and trapunto blocks with the side and corner setting triangles. (See "Diagonally Set Quilts" on page 86.) Join the blocks in each row. Press the seams in opposite directions from row to row.
Step 2. Join the rows, making sure to match the seams between blocks. Trim and square up the outside edges after the rows are sewn if needed.
Step 3. Add the borders as directed for borders with mitered corners on page 88.

Cording

Read these instructions entirely before beginning to cord.
Step 1. Place the quilt top face down on a flat surface. Open and finger-press all seams. Prepare channels for

cording by stitching each open seam to the quilt top, approximately 3/16" from the seam line. Use small running stitches. First, stitch the channels on each side of the seams that join the diagonal rows. (See step 2 of "Assembling the Quilt Top" on page 67.) This will make long, continuous channels.

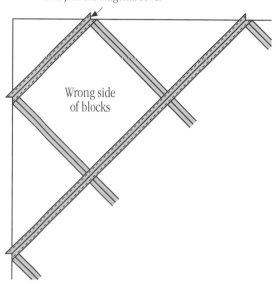

To make continuous channels, stitch 3/16" on each side of seams that join the diagonal rows.

Wrong side of blocks

Step 2. Stitch the other shorter diagonal channels. Do not cross the channels that you stitched in step 1.

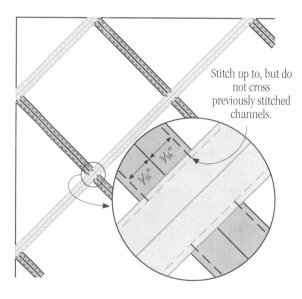

Stitch up to, but do not cross previously stitched channels.

Step 3. Next, stitch the channels on each side of the seams that join the border to the quilt top. Do not cross any previously stitched channels.

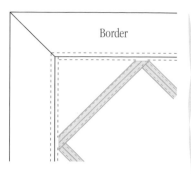

Border

Step 4. Thread the needle with 2 strands of yarn. You will pull 4 strands through the channels. *Do not* knot the yarn. Working on the back side, insert the needle between threads of the fabric as you did when stuffing. Gently pull the yarn through the stitched channel. Exit the needle on the same side of the work as you entered. (Refer to cording tip on page 40.) Clip the yarn close to the needle exit point and use the tip of the needle to poke the end of the yarn into the hole. Close the opening as you did when you completed the stuffing.

Cord the long channels first, using a trapunto needle. Then use a tapestry needle to cord the shorter ones.

✿ Finishing the Quilt

Step 1. Make the backing. Make sure it extends 2" beyond all edges of the quilt top.

Step 2. Layer the quilt top with batting and backing; baste.

Step 3. Quilt as desired or follow the quilting suggestion. Be sure to end your quilting 7/8" from the outside edge of the quilt to allow for finishing the seam and for 2 additional cording channels.

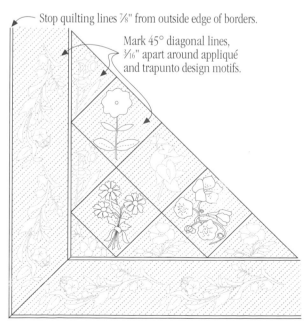

Stop quilting lines 7/8" from outside edge of borders.

Mark 45° diagonal lines, 3/16" apart around appliqué and trapunto design motifs.

Quilting Suggestion

Flowers of Brittany

Step 4. Trim the backing so that it is the same size as the quilt top. Trim the batting ¼" smaller than the quilt backing.

Step 5. Fold the quilt-top edge over the batting, onto the backing, turning under a ¼"-wide seam allowance. Turn the edge of the backing under a little more than ¼" and pin the backing turned edge to the quilt-top turned edge.

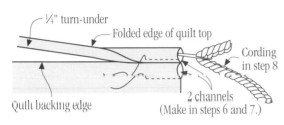

Step 6. Using small running stitches, sew the folded edges together through all the layers, approximately ³⁄₁₆" from the outer edge of the quilt. This finishes the edge of the quilt and creates a stitching line for the outermost cording channel.

Step 7. Finally, sew a line of running stitches ³⁄₁₆" from the stitching line made in step 6 above, to create another cording channel.

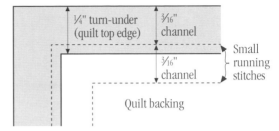

Step 8. Cord the 2 channels with yarn as you did before.

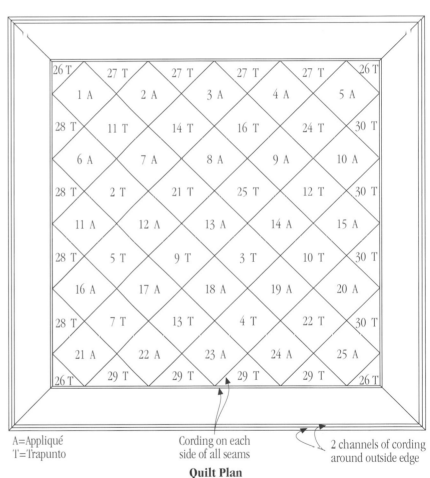

A=Appliqué
T=Trapunto

Cording on each side of all seams

2 channels of cording around outside edge

Quilt Plan

Flowers of Brittany

The Flowers of Brittany Patterns

#1 Hibiscus

#2 Iris

#3 Daffodil

#4 Red Poppy

#5 Morning Glory

#6 Primrose

#7 Anthurium

#8 Hydrangea

#9 Tulips

#10 Wild Rose

#11 Cornflower

#12 Mimosa

#13 Poppy

#14 Pansies

#15 Chrysanthemum

#16 Zinnia

#17 Anemone

#18 Camellia

#19 Dahlia

#20 Periwinkle

#21 Daisy

#22 Nasturtium

#23 Forget-me-not

#24 Magnolia

#25 Amaryllis

#26 Corner Setting Block

#27 Side Setting Block

#28 Side Setting Block

#29 Side Setting Block

#30 Side Setting Block

(Right) Le Rouvray, 1994 support beams are in place in preparation for foundation repairs.

(Below) *Le Rouvray,* by Cosabeth Parriaud, 1991, Paris, France, 3½" x 4⅜". Hand pieced and hand quilted.

Le Rouvray

Sometimes we give patterns to our clients. This one was offered at Christmastime. I made the stylized version of the entry to the original fortified farm, Le Rouvray, which was the inspiration for our logo.

Cosabeth Parriaud

LE ROUVRAY
PATCHWORK

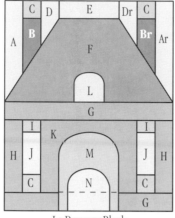

Finished block size: $3\frac{1}{2}$" x $4\frac{3}{8}$"

Materials

Scraps of red, green, and off-white prints and a green solid. (The block pictured includes an off-white print with metallic gold hearts.)

Le Rouvray Block
Finished size: $3\frac{1}{2}$" x $4\frac{3}{8}$"
Make 1.

Cutting

Make plastic templates of each template on page 73.

From the **red print**, cut:
　1 Template F
　1 Template M

From the **green print**, cut:
　2 Template G
　2 Template H
　2 Template I
　2 Template C
　1 Template K

From the **off-white** print, cut:
　1 Template A
　1 Template A reversed
　2 Template C
　1 Template D
　1 Template D reversed
　1 Template E
　2 Template J
　1 Template L
　1 Template N

From the **green solid**, cut:
　1 Template B
　1 Template B reversed

Assembling the Block

Step 1. Piece the block as shown.

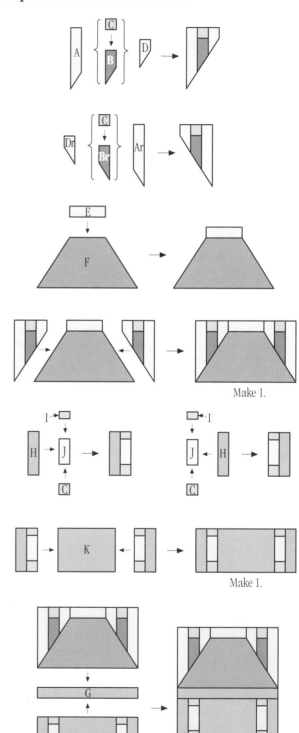

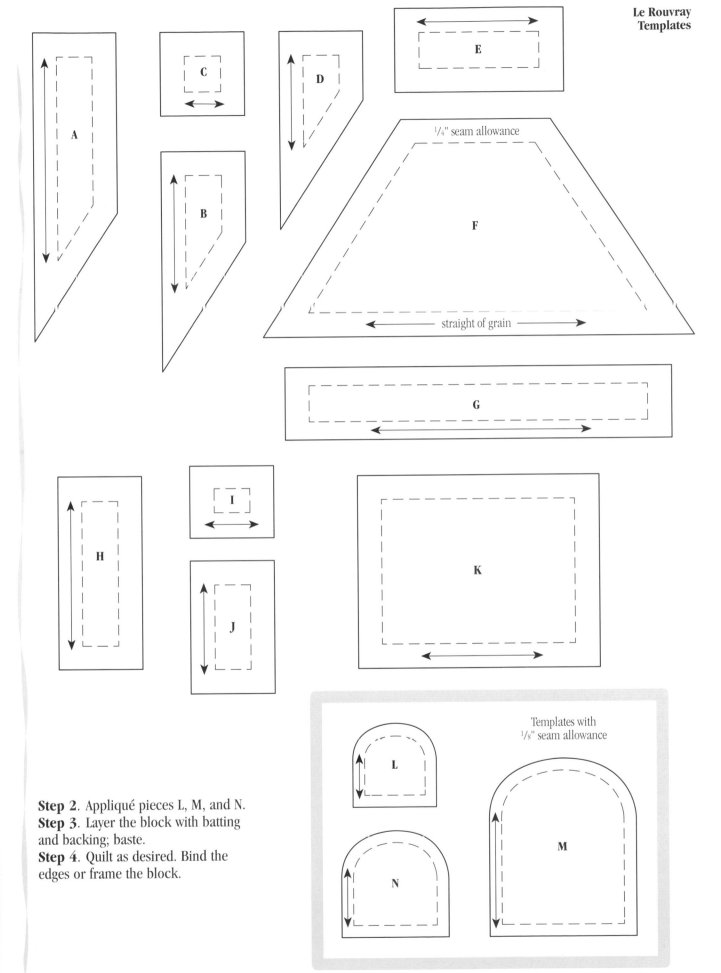

A

C

D

E

B

¼" seam allowance

F

straight of grain

G

H

I

J

K

Templates with
⅛" seam allowance

L

M

N

Step 2. Appliqué pieces L, M, and N.
Step 3. Layer the block with batting
and backing; baste.
Step 4. Quilt as desired. Bind the
edges or frame the block.

Le Rouvray

Slippers, by Joëlle de Bailliencourt, 1993, Paris, France. Machine pieced and machine quilted.

Slippers (pantoufles)

I've always made all my childrens' clothes. It was fun and economical as they were growing up. So, Timothée, Théophanie, Wanda, and Gédéon were dressed from head to . . . almost toe by Maman (mama). I made caps, coats, dresses, trousers . . . but what about the feet? I didn't feel that I could make shoes, so with leftover scraps from sewing projects, I made slippers. Eventually I made slippers for all my relatives.

Recently I decided to make them in patchwork, because it is my passion. Here is the result. I hope you like them. I used French Provençal fabrics, but use whatever scraps you have and improvise the piecing design.

Joëlle de Bailliencourt

The pattern is for women's size 8–9. Adjust to your size as necessary.

Materials: 44"-wide fabric

Scraps of a variety of fabrics
¼ yd. blue fabric
⅛ yd. thick batting
⅛ yd. muslin
2 yds. of 1½"-wide purchased prefolded bias binding

Cutting

Use the piecing design and pattern on page 76. Note on the pattern that the inside of the foot is indicated; therefore you will make one right and one left slipper.

From the **blue** fabric, cut:

    1 slipper top

    1 slipper top reversed

    2 each, slipper sole

    2 each, slipper sole reversed

From the **batting**, cut:

    2 slipper top

    2 slipper sole

From the **muslin**, cut:

    1 slipper top

    1 slipper top reversed

Making the Slippers

Use accurate ¼"-wide seam allowances.

Step 1. Trace the piecing lines onto the muslin slipper tops as shown on the piecing design. Use a pencil and be sure to make 1 and 1 reversed (one each for the right and left foot—note the inside of the foot on the pattern).

Step 2. All of the marked lines are the stitching lines. All fabric pieces (using your scraps of fabric) are positioned on the unmarked side of the muslin. Finger-press each piece open over the space it is to cover. Make sure that an adequate seam allowance extends into the adjacent areas. Add each piece in the numerical order indicated on the piecing design, to cover the slipper top. To reduce bulk, trim seam allowances to

⅛"–³⁄₁₆" wide. Turn the block over, fold the foundation back out of the way, then trim.

Step 3. Place the center block, right side up, on the unmarked side of the muslin. Make sure the edges of the center block extend into the adjacent areas. Pin in place. Place log #1 on top of the center block, right sides together, along the joining seam line. Make sure both fabrics extend at least ¼" beyond the seam lines.

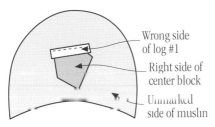

Wrong side of log #1

Right side of center block

Unmarked side of muslin

Step 4. Carefully turn the muslin over so that the marked side of the muslin is face up, holding the log and center block in place. Pin in place. Stitch on the line through the layers of the muslin and the 2 pieces.

Step 5. Finger-press log #1 open over the area it is to cover on the muslin. Trim the excess fabric, being careful to leave a seam allowance that extends into the adjacent areas.

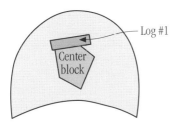

Log #1

Center block

Step 6. Add log #2, placing it on the center block, right sides together. Stitch. Finger-press and trim as you did before. Continue adding the logs in numerical order until the design is complete. Make one right and one left slipper top. Press the completed slipper tops and trim, following the shape of the muslin foundation.

Step 7. To complete the top part of the slippers, baste together the pieced top, batting, and backing. Quilt as desired.

Step 8. Bind the edge between points A and B (see slipper pattern) with the bias tape. Stitch the binding to the back side of the slipper top, then fold the binding to the pieced side of the top and topstitch along the edge as shown.

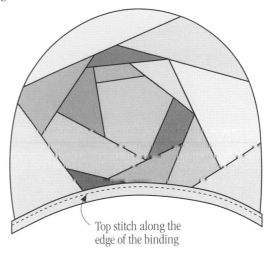

Top stitch along the edge of the binding

Step 9. To make the soles, baste a piece of batting between 2 blue fabric sole pieces. Machine quilt as shown. Make one right and one left slipper sole.

Step 10. Pin the slipper top on the sole, matching points A and B. Stitch them together.

Step 11. Bind the edges of the slipper with the bias binding as you did in step 8, being sure to sew through all layers.

TIP   Joëlle sometimes appliqués an extra sole to the slippers to make them last longer. She uses pieces of fabric cut from trousers that her children have outgrown.

Slippers

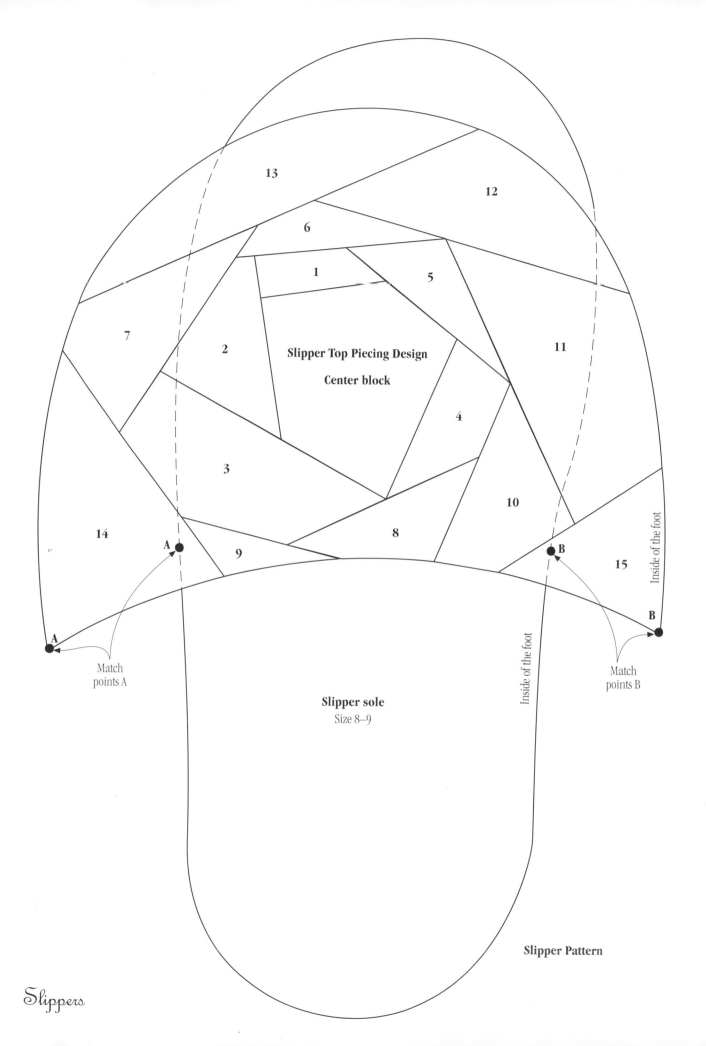

Slipper Top Piecing Design

Center block

13

12

6

1

5

7

2

11

4

3

10

14

A

A

9

8

B

B

15

Inside of the foot

Inside of the foot

Match points A

Match points B

Slipper sole
Size 8–9

Slipper Pattern

Quiltmaking Basics

Piecing

MAKING ACCURATE SEAMS

Precise and consistent ¼"-wide seams must be maintained to get the desired finished size of the quilt blocks. Use a ¼" quiltmaking presser foot on your sewing machine, or mark an accurate ¼" wide sewing guide on your machine. Use a ruler or graph paper with a ¼" grid to determine the measurement and mark the guide. Place a piece of masking tape or moleskin on the plate of the machine. Set the stitch length at 10 to 12 stitches per inch. Change your needle frequently. Backstitching is not necessary where seams will cross each other.

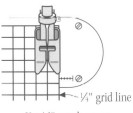
← ¼" grid line

Use ¼" graph paper to mark an accurate seam guide.

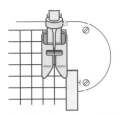
Put masking tape or moleskin in front of needle along edge of graph paper to guide fabric.

SET-IN SEAMS

Sometimes the only way to add a piece to a block is by stitching the piece into a corner. Set-in triangles and squares are added in two steps.

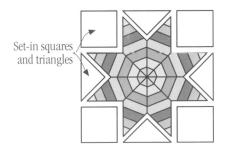

Set-in squares and triangles

Step 1. Mark the ¼" seam intersections at the outer corners and inside corner. Use your ruler to measure and mark ¼" cross hairs with a pencil at the seam intersections.

Set up three times a week, the bustling open-air market at Place Maubert has endured for centuries. Produce is grown in the South of France and Spain.

Step 2. Match the cross hairs of the triangle or square to the inside corner cross hairs of the block. The points should meet exactly. Use a pin to help guide you as you match the points. Pin in place. Fold or pin any other seams out of the way of the sewing area. Sew from the outer edge to the inside corner cross hairs. Do not sew past them.

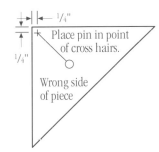
Place pin in point of cross hairs.

Wrong side of piece

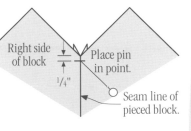
Right side of block — Place pin in point.

Seam line of pieced block.

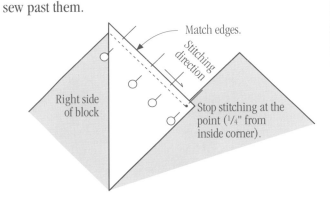
Match edges.

Stitching direction

Right side of block

Stop stitching at the point (¼" from inside corner).

Step 3. Pivot the remaining edge of the piece (triangle or square) to match the remaining edge of the block. Turn over and pin in place. Sew from the inside corner to the outer edge. Be careful not to catch any part of the other seam when stitching the second side. Press.

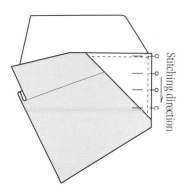

PRESSING

Generally, the rule in quiltmaking is to press seams to one side, toward the darker color whenever possible. Press the seam flat from the wrong side first, then press the seam in the desired direction from the right side. Press carefully to avoid distorting the shapes.

When joining two seamed units, plan ahead and press the seam allowances in opposite directions as shown. Not only does this make it easier to match seam lines, but it reduces bulk. The seam allowances will butt against each other where two seams meet, and seam intersections will match perfectly.

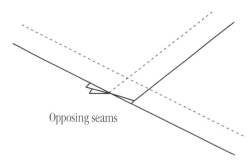

Opposing seams

MAKING BIAS SQUARES

Squares made from two contrasting half-square triangles are used in many quilt designs. These are called bias squares or half-square triangle units. There are different methods for making these units.

Using the bias strip-piecing method is an easy way to make large numbers of bias squares. This method is very accurate because seams are pressed right after the strips are pieced and before squares are cut. Instructions follow for making half-square triangle units using Mary Hickey's bias-square method as first

shown in her book *Angle Antics* (That Patchwork Place).

When you need only a small number of units or units in several different combinations, follow the instructions for "Cut and Pieced Squares" on page 79. Remember that this method requires careful pressing after squares are stitched and cut.

BIAS STRIP-PIECING METHOD

You will need a Bias Square® ruler to cut the units.
Step 1. Layer the two fabrics with right sides facing up. The directions for each quilt indicate how many and what size fabric pieces you need.
Step 2. Establish a true bias line on the top fabric, using a ruler with a 45°-angle line. Cut bias strips parallel to the drawn line. Each quilt plan requiring bias squares indicates how many strips to cut and how wide to cut them.

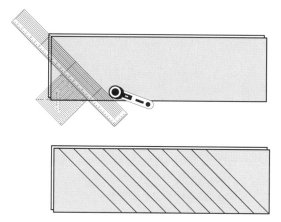

Step 3. Sew the strips together along the bias edges, offsetting the tops of the strips ¼" as shown. Alternating the fabrics, sew the strips into units of six to eight strips. Press seams toward the darker strips. When making 1½" or smaller bias squares, press seams open to distribute the bulk.

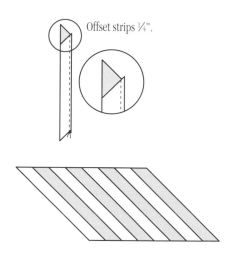

Offset strips ¼".

Quiltmaking Basics

Step 4. Position the Bias Square with the diagonal line on a seam line. Place a long ruler across the top to cut an even edge. The trimmed edge should be at a perfect 45° angle to the seam lines.

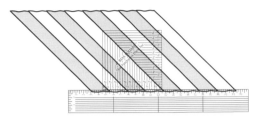

Step 5. Cut a segment parallel to the first cut. Each quilt plan specifies how wide to cut this segment. Continue cutting segments into the specified widths, making sure to check and correct the angle at the edge after each cut.

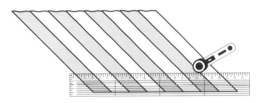

Step 6. Sew the segments together, end to end, to create a long strip-pieced unit. This method prevents wasting fabric at the end of each unit. Be careful not to stretch the bias edges as you sew.

Step 7. Place the Bias Square with the diagonal line on the seam line and one edge of the square on the bottom edge of the strip. Cut one side.

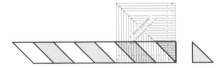

Step 8. Place the diagonal line of the Bias Square on the seam line and the bottom edge of the ruler on the cut edge of the strip and cut the next bias square. The edges of the square should line up with the markings on the ruler to cut the required-size squares.

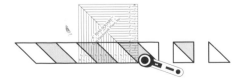

Step 9. Continue cutting squares across the remainder of the strip until you have the number of bias squares required for the quilt you are making. Remember to align the diagonal line on the ruler with the seam line before each cut.

Step 10. Measure your bias squares to make sure they are all the correct size. It may be necessary to carefully trim them to the correct size. Position the Bias Square with the diagonal line on the seam line and the required-size markings. Trim.

Trim away excess, if necessary.

CUT-AND-PIECED SQUARES

Use this method when you need only a small number of half-square triangle units, or you need units in several different fabric combinations.

Press carefully to avoid distorting the half-square triangle units.

Step 1. Cut squares the size indicated in the quilt plan.

Step 2. Draw a diagonal line from corner to corner on the back of the lightest fabric.

Step 3. Place the square with the drawn line on top of another square, right sides together. Sew ¼" away from the drawn line on both sides.

Step 4. Cut on the drawn line. Press the seams toward the darker fabric and trim the "dog-ear" corners. Each pair of squares you sew together yields two half-square triangle units.

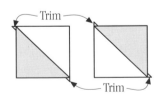

Trim

Trim

🐦 Basic Appliqué Techniques

MAKING TEMPLATES

Templates made from clear plastic are more durable and accurate than those made from cardboard. It is also easier to trace the templates accurately because you can see through the plastic.

Place template plastic over each pattern piece and trace with a fine-line permanent marker. Do not add seam allowances. Cut out the templates on the drawn lines. Mark the pattern name or piece number and the grain-line arrow (if necessary) on the template.

MARKING AND CUTTING FABRIC

Place the template right side up on the right side of the fabric. Leave at least ½" between tracings if more than one piece is needed. Cut out each piece, adding a scant ¼"-wide seam allowance around each tracing. The seam allowance will be turned under to create the finished edge of the appliqué. You may wish to add only ⅛"-wide seam allowances on tiny pieces.

Cut the background fabric the size and shape required for each project, adding an extra inch all around. Trim it to the correct size after the appliqué has been completed.

Place the background square or rectangle right side up over the pattern so that the design is centered. Trace the design lightly with a pencil. If your background fabric is dark, use a light table or tape the pattern to a window on a sunny day.

TRADITIONAL APPLIQUÉ METHOD

Step 1. Using a plastic template, trace the design onto the right side of the appliqué fabric.

Step 2. Cut out the fabric piece, adding a scant ¼"–wide (³⁄₁₆"– ¼") seam allowance all around.

Step 3. To get smoothly curved edges, clip inside points and the seam allowance on inside curves. Clip up to, but not across, the stitching line.

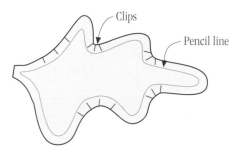

Clips

Pencil line

Step 4. Turn under the seam allowance, rolling the traced line to the back. Do not turn under edges that will be covered by other appliqué pieces. They should lie flat under the covering piece. Baste around the fabric piece.

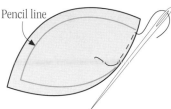

Pencil line

Step 5. Position the appliqué piece on the background fabric; pin or baste in place.

NEEDLE-TURN APPLIQUÉ METHOD

With this method, you do not turn under and baste the seam allowances prior to appliqué.

Annick, who made the "Flowers of Brittany" quilt on page 66, prefers this method of appliqué; however, she only adds a ⅛"-wide seam allowance when she cuts her appliqué pieces.

Step 1. Using a plastic template, trace the design onto the right side of the appliqué fabric.

Step 2. Cut out the fabric piece, adding a scant ¼"-wide (³⁄₁₆"– ¼") seam allowance all around.

Step 3. Position the appliqué piece on the background fabric; pin or baste in place.

Step 4. Starting on a straight edge, use the tip of the needle to gently turn under the seam allowance, about ½" at a time. Hold the turned seam allowance firmly between the thumb and first finger of your left hand (reverse if you are left-handed) as you stitch the appliqué to the background. Use a longer needle, such as a "Sharp" or milliner's needle, to help you turn the seam allowance under neatly.

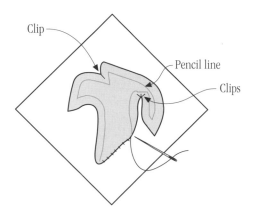

Clip

Pencil line

Clips

PAPER-PATCH APPLIQUÉ METHOD

Make a paper template of each appliqué shape. Do not add seam allowances. Use freezer paper, white kraft paper, or white bond-weight paper.

Step 1. Pin the paper patches to the wrong side of the appliqué fabric.

Step 2. Cut out the appliqué shapes, adding a ¼"-wide seam allowance all around.

Step 3. Turn the seam allowance over onto the paper and baste it to the paper. Clip any inside points and the seam allowance on curves. Baste close to the edge.

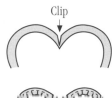
Clip

See pages 82–83 for preparing and stitching leaves, flowers, and flower centers.

NOTE: Do not turn under edges that will be covered by other appliqué pieces. They should lie flat under the covering appliqué piece.

Step 4. After pressing the prepared appliqué shapes, place them on the background fabric. Baste or pin them in place. If you have trouble with thread tangling around the pins as you sew, pin from the underside of your work.

Step 5. Using a small blind stitch and a single matching thread, appliqué the pieces to the background. Match your thread to each appliqué shape. Space the stitches evenly, ¹⁄₁₆"–⅛" apart. Pieces that lie under other pieces must be sewn in place first.

Step 6. After all shapes have been stitched to the background fabric, remove the basting stitches. Turn the block over to the wrong side and cut a small slit in the background fabric behind the appliqué. Remove the paper templates with tweezers. If you prefer, trim away the background fabric to within ⅛"–¼" of the stitching line. Be careful not to clip the appliqué stitches.

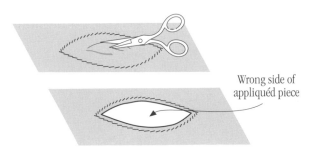
Wrong side of appliquéd piece

TRADITIONAL APPLIQUÉ STITCH

The blind stitch or traditional appliqué stitch is appropriate for sewing all appliqué shapes.

Step 1. Tie a knot in a single strand of thread that is approximately 18" long.

Step 2. Hide the knot by slipping the needle into the seam allowance from the wrong side of the appliqué piece; bring the needle out on the fold line.

Step 3. Work from right to left if you are right-handed, or from left to right if you are left-handed.

Step 4. Start the first stitch by moving the needle straight off the appliqué, inserting the needle into the background fabric. Let the needle travel under the background fabric, parallel to the edge of the appliqué, bringing it up about ⅛" away, along the pattern line.

Step 5. As you bring the needle up, pierce the edge of the appliqué piece, catching only one or two threads of the folded edge.

Step 6. Move the needle straight off the appliqué into the background fabric. Let your needle travel under the background, bringing it up about ⅛" away, again catching the edge of the appliqué.

Step 7. Give the thread a slight tug and continue stitching.

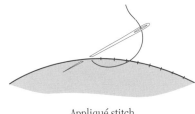
Appliqué stitch

Quiltmaking Basics

Step 8. To end your stitching, pull the needle through to the wrong side. Behind the appliqué piece, take two small stitches, making knots by taking your needle through the loops. Check the right side to see if the thread "shadows" through your background. If it does, take one more small stitch on the back side to direct the tail of the thread under the appliqué fabric so that it won't show through to the right side.

APPLIQUÉ STEMS

Use metal or heat-resistant nylon press bars, or make a pressing template the finished width of the stem from card stock. Make long "tubes" of stems and cut them to the required lengths as you appliqué.

Step 1. Cut bias strips the finished width of the stem, plus ½" for seam allowances.

Step 2. Place the fabric on your ironing board, right side down. Center the press bar or template on the fabric. Press one side of the fabric over the bar, then the other to make a "tube." Remove the bar.

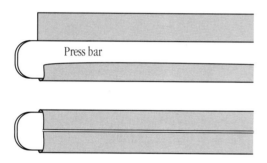

Press bar

Step 3. Cut the required stem lengths from the stem "tube" as you need them. Place the folded edges of the stem on the penciled placement lines of your background fabric. Stitch in place. If the block requires curved stems, stitch the inside curve in place first and then the outside curve.

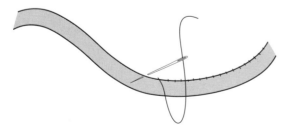

APPLIQUÉ LEAVES

Step 1. Turn the point in toward the leaf, then fold the two sides in to form the point. Trim excess seam allowance to eliminate bulky points.

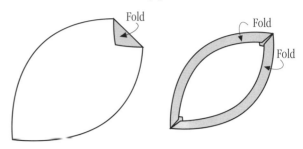

Fold — Fold — Fold

Step 2. As you baste along curves, keep the stitches close to the fold to keep the shape accurate.

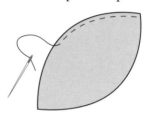

Step 3. As you appliqué, start taking smaller stitches within ½" of the point. Smaller stitches near the point keep any frayed edges of the seam allowance from escaping. Place stitches on either side of the point to accent the point. Do not put a stitch directly on the point as it will flatten it.

APPLIQUÉ FLOWERS

Step 1. Carefully clip the seam allowance between the "petals." Clip to within two or three threads of the inner point to eliminate frayed threads between the petals.

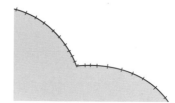

Clip

Step 2. As you appliqué, use the tip of the needle to push under the threads and take tiny stitches at the inner points to control the threads.

FLOWER CENTERS OR CIRCLES

Step 1. Cut circle templates the exact size of the finished circle from heavy paper, such as a manila file folder.

Step 2. Trace around the template onto the fabric. Cut the circles from the fabric, adding ¼" around the edge of the template.

Step 3. Sew with a small running stitch around the fabric circle. Keep the stitches within the seam allowance but not too close to the edge.

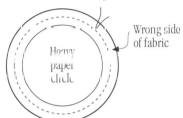

Wrong side of fabric

Heavy paper circle

Step 4. Place the paper template in the center of the wrong side of the fabric circle. Pull the thread ends to draw the seam allowance in around the template.

Step 5. Steam-press the circle, then let it cool a minute or two. Carefully peel back the fabric and remove the paper circle. Gently pull the basting threads to tighten the seam allowance and make it lie flat.

Step 6. Pin the circle in place and appliqué with tiny stitches.

RAISED APPLIQUÉ

Raised appliqué is made by quilting a layer of batting to the appliqué piece, then appliquéing the quilted shape to the background fabric.

Step 1. Cut the fabric piece, adding a ³⁄₁₆"-wide seam allowance. Trace the quilting pattern onto the right side of the appliqué piece.

Step 2. Cut the batting to the exact shape and size of the appliqué template.

Step 3. Following the quilting pattern, quilt the two layers.

Step 4. Appliqué the quilted piece in place, using the needle-turn technique. (See page 80.)

GATHERED FLOWERS

Gathered flowers add a special three-dimensional look (and feel) to appliqué designs. Use Mimi Dietrich's technique and marking guide for "ruching" as first shown in her book *Baltimore Bouquets* (That Patchwork Place).

Step 1. Cut a straight-grain strip of fabric 1⅝" x 25".

Step 2. Fold the strip in half along the long side, right sides together. Sew the two edges together with small stitches, using a ¼"-wide seam allowance. Trim the seam to a scant ⅛".

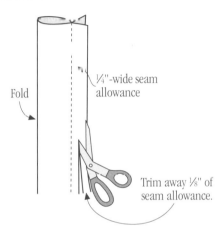

Fold

¼"-wide seam allowance

Trim away ⅛" of seam allowance.

Step 3. Turn the strip right side out. Press the strip flat, with the seam in the center back of the strip. Lay the strip right side up on the guide below. Use a fabric marker to place dots on the folded edges of your strip at 1" intervals. Mark the entire length of the strip. Use the marking guide at the bottom of this page.

Step 4. Using a gathering stitch, hand sew a zigzag line connecting the marked dots. Start at one end of the strip, bring your needle out through the bottom folded edge, then take two or three small stitches on the fold to lock the thread. Stitch from dot to dot, taking a stitch over the folded edge when you change direction.

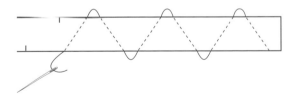

After stitching about 8", pull the thread to gather the fabric. Pull the thread in a straight line, gathering fabric petals on each side. Pull the thread tight, then adjust

Marking guide for gathering flower

the fabric to spread the petals slightly. Continue stitching until you have 21 petals on each edge.

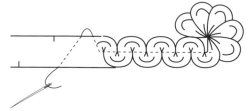

Step 5. With a second needle and thread, form the flower. First, trim the starting edge to ¼". Turn the seam allowance under the first petal and tack it securely. Arrange the first five petals into a circle, then take a stitch in the first five "inside" petals to draw them together.

Carefully arrange the sixth petal slightly under the first one to begin making a second row of petals. Turn the flower to the wrong side and tack the inside petals to the back (¼" inside the edge) as you form the flower.

When you get to the end of the flower, taper the last petal under the first row, adjusting it to form a smooth shape. You may need to add a few petals.

As you finish, your gathering stitches should stop on the outside edge of the strip. Pull the thread to make the last petal and knot the thread. Cut the strip ¼" beyond the last stitch, then slip the raw edges under the previous row.

After the flower is formed, start at the outside edge and appliqué the petals securely to the background fabric. Stitch the center edge of each petal and each inner point. Your stitches will move in a spiral toward the center of the flower.

BRAIDED RICKRACK FLOWERS

Annick made this flower to add a special look to her Camelia block (Block #18, page 70). Use one 45" length each of two values of large rickrack.

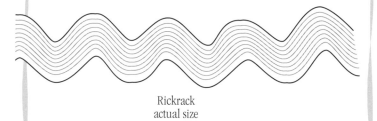

Rickrack
actual size

Step 1. Pin one end of each length of rickrack together. Then begin "braiding" or interlocking the two lengths together.

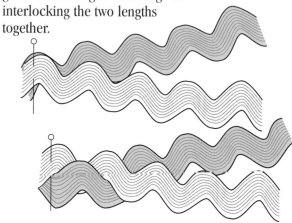

Step 2. After you have interlocked a 3" length of the two rickracks together, bring the pinned starting end around to overlap the just-interlocked end. Pin in place, tucking the raw edges of the rickrack ends underneath. Turn the piece over and tack the interlocked rickrack together, using a coordinating color of thread. Be careful that your stitches do not show through to the right side of the flower. This forms the center of the flower.

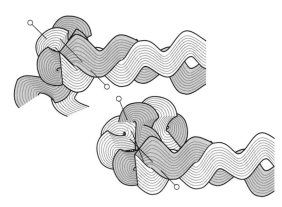

Step 3. Continue interlocking the two lengths of rickrack and adding to the flower center, working from the center out. Tack the layers together as you go.

Wrong side of flower

Step 4. When your camelia is the same size as the template, trim off the excess lengths of rickrack, place the raw edges on the back side of the flower, and tack them down. Appliqué the flower to your block.

Quiltmaking Basics

Trapunto

Trapunto is similar to boutis, but there are some differences. Trapunto is completed block by block or element by element, using a loosely woven fabric, such as muslin, for the backing. Trapunto, unlike boutis, is made as a quilt top, which will later be layered with batting and backing.

Step 1. Place the pattern under the white fabric block. Trace the entire trapunto design onto the fabric. Use a sharp, medium-lead pencil. These lines, when stitched, form the motifs that will be stuffed or corded.

Step 2. Baste the two layers (white fabric and lining) together.

Step 3. Place the block loosely in an embroidery hoop.

The most famous bakery in the world, Poilâne, bakes bread in wood-fired ovens and flies loaves to expensive gourmet shops in New York and Tokyo. Bon appétit!

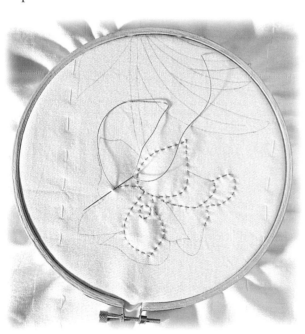

Step 4. Starting in the center, sew the two layers together with small running stitches. Stitch all of the design motifs before stuffing. (As in quilting, hide the thread knot between the two layers of fabric.) Take the work out of the hoop.

Step 5. To stuff the motifs, turn work to the back and separate the threads of the lining with a needle or an orange stick. Fill each area of the design motifs with synthetic batting, using an orange stick. Do not overstuff or understuff; the areas should be full but not firm. Check the front side as you work to make sure that the stuffing is even and does not pucker. Close the

openings by scratching the surface of the muslin with your needle or orange stick.

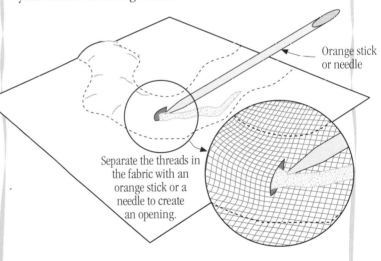

Orange stick or needle

Separate the threads in the fabric with an orange stick or a needle to create an opening.

Step 6. When trapunto is completed, carefully trim away the excess lining fabric, leaving approximately ¼" around the motifs. The block is now ready to be assembled into a quilt top.

Assembling the Quilt Top

SQUARING UP BLOCKS

After completing your blocks, take the time to square them up. Use a large square ruler to measure them and make sure they are the desired size plus an extra ¼" all around for seam allowances. After measuring them all, trim the larger blocks to match the size of the smallest one. Be sure to trim all the sides.

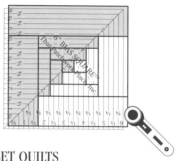

The St. Germain quarter is the home of a plethora of artists' ateliers, art galleries, antique shops, and cafés. Vignettes in display windows lure you inside.

STRAIGHT-SET QUILTS

Step 1. Arrange the blocks as shown in the quilt plan provided with each quilt.
Step 2. Sew the blocks together in horizontal rows; press the seams in opposite directions from row to row.
Step 3. Sew the rows together, making sure to match the seams between the blocks.

The sizes of the side and corner triangles for the quilts in this book are provided; however, for detailed instructions on how to calculate sizes for side and corner triangles, refer to *Rotary Riot* by Judy Hopkins and Nancy J. Martin (That Patchwork Place).

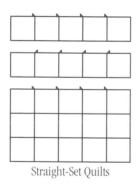

Straight-Set Quilts

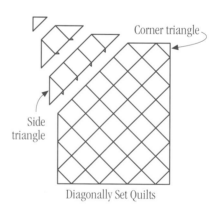

Corner triangle

Side triangle

Diagonally Set Quilts

DIAGONALLY SET QUILTS

Step 1. Arrange the blocks, side triangles, and corner triangles as shown in the quilt plan provided with each quilt.
Step 2. Sew the blocks together in diagonal rows; press the seams in opposite directions from row to row.
Step 3. Sew the rows together, making sure to match the seams between the blocks. Sew the corner triangles on last.

Quiltmaking Basics

Adding Borders

Borders add a finishing touch to a quilt because they contain the design and draw the eye into the quilt. Always measure the quilt first, before adding border strips. The edges of a quilt are often slightly longer than the distance through the center, due to stretching during construction. By measuring first, you are assured of having a finished quilt that is as straight as possible.

Generally, plain border strips are cut along the crosswise grain and seamed where necessary to gain the required length. Seaming is not necessary when cutting borders from the lengthwise grain of fabric; however, extra fabric is required.

Add borders that have straight-cut corners, corner squares, or mitered corners.

STRAIGHT-CUT BORDERS

Step 1. Measure the length of the quilt top through the center. Cut border strips to that measurement, piecing as necessary. If you have already cut strips, trim them to that measurement. Mark the center of the quilt edges and the border strips. Pin the borders to the sides of the quilt top, matching the center marks and ends and easing as necessary. Sew the border strips in place. Press seams toward the border.

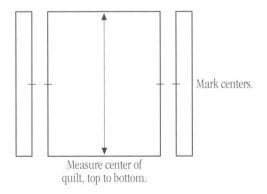

Mark centers.

Measure center of quilt, top to bottom.

Step 2. Measure the width of the quilt top through the center, including the side borders just added. Cut border strips to that measurement, piecing as necessary. If you have already cut strips, trim them to that measurement. Mark the center of the quilt edges and the border strips. Pin the borders to the top and bottom edges of the quilt top, matching the center

marks and ends and easing as necessary. Sew the border strips in place. Press seams toward the border.

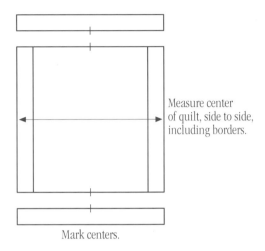

Measure center of quilt, side to side, including borders.

Mark centers.

BORDERS WITH CORNER SQUARES

Step 1. Measure the width and length of the quilt top through the center. Cut border strips to those measurements, piecing as necessary. Mark the center of the quilt edges and the border strips. Pin the side borders to the sides of the quilt top, matching the center marks and ends and easing as necessary. Sew the border strips in place. Press seams toward the border.

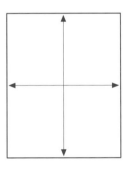

Louis XIV (the "Sun King") created a splendid palace and beautiful gardens at Versailles. Today Versailles offers a feast of quilters' inspirations.

Step 2. Cut corner squares of the required size (the cut width of the border strips). Sew one corner square to each end of the remaining two border strips; press seams toward the border strips. Pin the border strips to the top and bottom edges of the quilt top. Match centers, seams between the border strip and corner square, and ends, easing as necessary. Sew the border strips in place. Press seams toward the border.

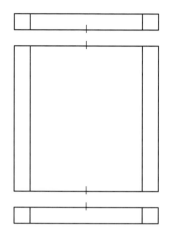

MITERED BORDERS

Step 1. Estimate the finished outside dimensions of your quilt, including borders. Border strips should be cut to this length plus at least ½" for seam allowances; it is safer to add 3"– 4" to give yourself leeway. For example, if your quilt measures 45½" x 50½" across the center and you want a 5"-wide finished border, your quilt will measure 55" x 60" after the border is attached.

NOTE: If your quilt has multiple borders, sew the individual strips together and treat the resulting unit as a single border strip.

Step 2. Mark the center of the quilt edges and the border strips.
Step 3. Measure the length and width of the quilt top across the center. Note the measurements.
Step 4. Place a pin at each end of the side border strips to mark the length of the quilt top. Repeat with the top and bottom borders.

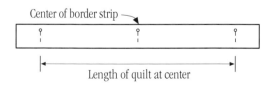

Step 5. Pin the borders to the quilt top, matching the centers. Line up the pins at either end of the border strip with the edges of the quilt. Sew in place, begin-

ning and ending the stitching ¼" from the raw edges of the quilt top. Repeat with the remaining borders.

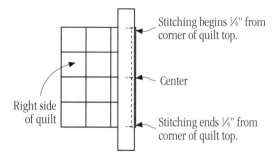

Step 6. Lay the first corner to be mitered on your ironing board. Fold under one border strip at a 45° angle to the other strip. Press and pin.

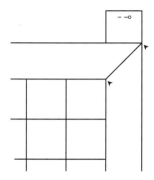

Step 7. Fold the quilt with right sides together, lining up the edges of the border. If necessary, use a ruler to draw a pencil line on the crease to make the line more visible. Sew on the pressed crease, stitching from the corner to the outside edge.

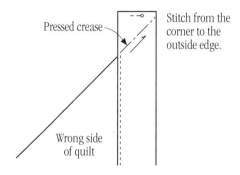

Step 8. Press the seam open and trim away excess border strips, leaving a ¼"-wide seam allowance.
Step 9. Repeat with remaining corners.

Quiltmaking Basics

✿ Marking the Quilting Design

Press your quilt top. Mark the quilting design on the quilt top, whether you hand or machine quilt, unless you are stitching in-the-ditch, outlining the design ¼" away from all seams, or stitching a grid of straight lines, using ¼"-wide masking tape as a guide. Don't leave tape on a quilt top for an extended length of time because the tape may leave a sticky residue.

Quilting-in-the-Ditch   Outline Quilting

Quilting Grids

• To quilt in-the-ditch, place the stitches in the valley created next to the seam. Stitch on the side that does not have the seam allowance under it.

• To outline a design, stitch ¼" away from the seam inside each shape. You can quilt without marking the line, or use ¼"-wide masking tape.

• To mark a grid or pattern of lines that are ¼" apart, use ¼"-wide masking tape in 15"–18" lengths. Place strips of tape on the quilt top and quilt next to the edge of the tape. Remove the tape when stitching is complete. Reuse the tape to mark another area.

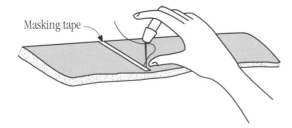

Masking tape

Even graceful details in this old brass door handle evoke a classic quilting design.

To mark other quilting designs, use a stencil or trace a design onto the quilt top, using a light table, before it is layered with the batting and backing. Use stencils to mark repeated designs. Marking pens and pencils are available in a variety of colors. Always draw the lines lightly and always test markers on a scrap of fabric to be sure that the lines can be removed.

89

Quiltmaking Basics

 Layering the Quilt

Make your quilt backing at least 3"– 4" larger than the quilt top all the way around. For a large quilt, you will usually need to sew two or three lengths of fabric together to make a backing of the required size. Trim away the selvages before piecing the lengths together. Press the backing seams open to make quilting easier. Save leftover fabric for another quilt project. If you find fabric wider than 44", you may not need as many lengths to make the backing.

Two lengths of fabric seamed in the center

1 fabric width

Partial fabric width

It is always a good idea to unroll your batting and let it relax overnight before you layer your quilt. Be sure to check the manufacturer's instructions for any prewashing directions, prior to layering your quilt. After the batting has relaxed, cut it at least 2" larger than the quilt top all the way around.

Step 1. Spread the backing, wrong side up, on a flat, clean surface. Anchor it with pins or masking tape. Be careful not to stretch the backing out of shape.

Step 2. Spread the batting over the backing, smoothing out any wrinkles.

Step 3. Place the pressed quilt top on top of the batting. Smooth out any wrinkles and make sure the edges of the quilt top are parallel to the edges of the backing.

Step 4. Starting in the center, baste with needle and thread and work diagonally to each corner. Continue basting in a grid of horizontal and vertical lines 6"–8" apart. Finish by basting around the edges. When you are quilting, you may find that you will need to remove the basting from the edges in order to smooth out wrinkles that occur during quilting. Remove the masking tape after you have completed the basting.

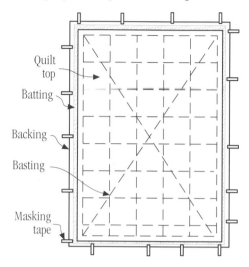

Quilt top

Batting

Backing

Basting

Masking tape

Note: If you plan to machine quilt, you may baste the layers with #2 rustproof safety pins. Place pins about 6"–8" apart, away from the area you plan to quilt.

Above the portals on the west façade of Notre Dame is the Gallery of Kings. These medieval masterpieces peek out behind the layers of scaffolding, which is in place for the cleaning and repair of the cathedral.

Hand Quilting

Hand quilting adds a special touch to your quilt. Once you establish a stitching rhythm, it is a relaxing activity. You will need quilting thread, short quilting needles (called Betweens), and a thimble. Many quilters find that using a quilting hoop or frame helps to keep the work smooth and even.

Step 1. Thread your needle with a single strand of quilting thread, about 18" long. Make a small, single knot at the end of the thread.

Step 2. Insert the needle in the top layer about 1" from where you want to start stitching. Pull the needle out at the point where quilting will begin and gently pull the thread until the knot pops through the fabric and into the batting.

Step 3. Take small, evenly spaced stitches through all three quilt layers.

Step 4. Rock the needle up and down through all layers until you have three or four stitches on the needle. Place your other hand underneath the quilt so you can feel the point of the needle with the tip of your finger when a stitch is taken.

Step 5. To end a line of quilting, make a small knot close to the last stitch. Then, backstitch, running the thread a needle's length through the batting. Gently pull the thread until the knot pops into the batting; clip the thread at the quilt's surface.

The carousel at the base of the steps to Sacré-Coeur in Place St. Pierre is a very popular spot when children get out of school.

For more techniques on hand quilting, refer to *Loving Stitches* by Jeana Kimball (That Patchwork Place).

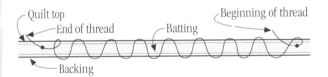

Quilt top — End of thread — Batting — Beginning of thread — Backing

Many of the streets in the neighborhood around Le Rouvray date from the Middle Ages. Every day the streets and sidewalks are flushed with water and swept by *caninettes*—motorbikes equipped with rotating brushes and suction hoses.

Binding

Binding can be made from bias or straight-grain strips of fabric. Most of the quilts in this book are bound with straight-grain binding.

Another method for finishing the edges without making a separate binding is to simply turn the backing fabric over the batting onto the quilt top and finish the edge.

STRAIGHT-GRAIN BINDING

The finished width (on the top of the quilt) of straight-grain binding for most of the projects in this book is between ¼" and ⅜" wide, depending on the loft of the batting.

Cut 1¼"-wide strips across the width of the fabric. Cut enough strips to go around the perimeter of the quilt plus 10" for seams and corners in a mitered fold. Trim the ends of the strips at a 45° angle and seam the ends to make one long piece of binding.

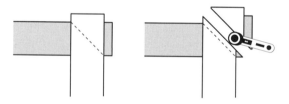

From the Eiffel Tower (Tour Eiffel), you can see the Parc du Champs de Mars, which has been a site of many battles. In 52 B.C. Parisians lost a battle with Roman legions, and in A.D. 886 Parisians held their territory against invading Vikings.

BIAS BINDING

Make a bias cut in a length of fabric, starting at one corner and using the 45°-angle marking on a long cutting ruler as a guide. Cut 2½"-wide bias strips (which finish to a ⅜"-wide binding), measuring from the first bias cut. Seam the ends to make one long piece of binding. Press the seams open. Fold the seamed binding strip in half lengthwise, wrong sides together, and press.

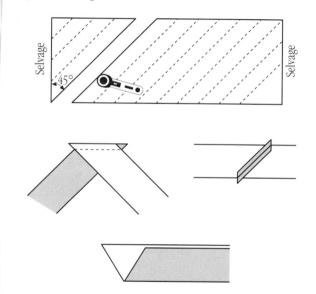

Estimated Bias Yield

Bias Binding Fabric	Yields Approximately
¼ yd.	125"
⅜ yd.	200"
½ yd.	275"
⅝ yd.	350"
¾ yd.	440"

ATTACHING THE BINDING

Step 1. Turn under ¼" at a 45° angle at one end of the strip and press.

Fold line

Quiltmaking Basics

Step 2. Trim batting and backing even with the quilt top.

Step 3. For bias binding, starting on one side of the quilt and using a ³⁄₈"-wide seam allowance, sew the binding to the quilt, keeping the raw edges even with the quilt-top edge. End the stitching ³⁄₈" from the corner of the quilt and backstitch. Clip the thread.

For straight-grain binding, place the binding on the quilt top, right sides together, aligning the raw edges of the binding with the quilt-top edge. Use a ¼"-wide seam allowance to sew the binding to the quilt. End the stitching ¼" from the corner of the quilt and backstitch. Clip the thread.

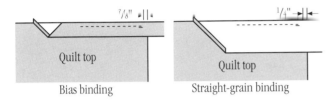

Bias binding Straight-grain binding

Step 4. Turn the quilt so that you will be stitching down the next side. Fold the binding up, away from the quilt.

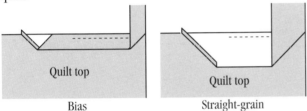

Bias Straight-grain

Step 5. Fold the binding back down onto itself, parallel with the edge of the quilt top. Begin sewing at the edge, backstitching to secure the stitching at the edge. Repeat on the remaining edges and corners of the quilt.

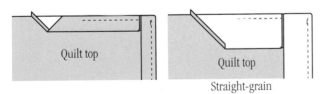

Quilt top Quilt top

Straight-grain

Step 6. When you reach the beginning of the binding, overlap the beginning stitches by about 1" and cut away any excess binding, trimming the end at a 45° angle. Tuck the end of the binding into the fold and finish the seam.

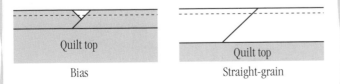

Bias Straight-grain

Step 7. Fold the binding over the raw edges of the quilt to the back. For bias binding, place the folded edge so that it covers the row of machine stitching; blindstitch in place. For straight-grain binding, fold the remaining raw edge under ¼", then place the folded edge to cover the row of machine stitching; blindstitch in place. A miter will form at each corner. Blindstitch the mitered corners in place.

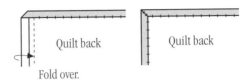

Quilt back Quilt back

Fold over.

SELF-BINDING (FINISHING WITH BACKING)

You can get two different effects on the front of the quilt. One is to simply "bind" the edges of the quilt, and the other is to make a "border" at the same time as finishing the edges. Either way, your backing must be larger than the quilt top.

To determine the size to make the backing, measure the quilt top as directed on page 87, then add two times your desired border width all around, plus seam allowances. Add a little extra to give yourself leeway. Remember that your batting must be wide enough to accommodate the width of the binding/border all the way around as well.

For example, if your quilt top measures 45½" x 50½" across the center and you want a 5"-wide finished "border," make your backing 66½" x 71½". For a finished "binding" width of ½", add 1½"–2" all the way around.

Step 1. After completing the quilting, trim batting even with the quilt top.

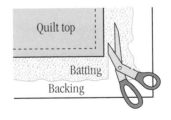

Quilt top

Batting

Backing

Step 2. *For a finished "binding" width of ½",* trim the backing carefully, leaving 1" of backing extending beyond all edges of the quilt top.

For finished *"binding"* or *"borders"* wider

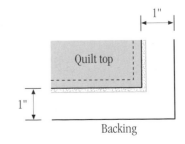

Quilt top

Backing

than ½", carefully trim away the "leeway" fabric that you added when you layered the quilt to quilt it. At this time, you only need to have two times the desired finished binding or border width plus ¼" all around for seam allowances.

Step 3. Fold the backing in half over to the front so that it overlaps the quilt top by ½" all around.

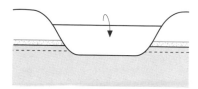

Step 4. Turn under a ¼"-wide seam allowance to form a finished edge. Pin and blindstitch in place. Either overlap the corners or make mitered corners as shown below.

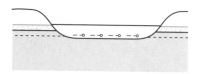

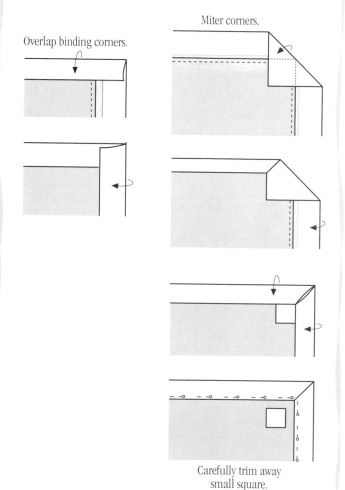

Overlap binding corners.

Miter corners.

Carefully trim away
small square.

Yardage Conversion Chart

FABRIC WIDTH			
44"–45"	50"	52"–54"	58"–60"
YARDAGE			
1⅜	1¼	1⅛	1
1⅝	1½	1⅜	1¼
1¾	1⅝	1½	1⅜
2⅛	1¾	1¾	1⅝
2¼	2	1⅞	1¾
2½	2¼	2	1⅞
2¾	2⅜	2¼	2
2⅞	2⅝	2⅜	2¼
3⅛	2¾	2⅝	2⅜
3⅜	3	2¾	2⅝
3⅝	3¼	2⅞	2¾
3⅞	3⅜	3⅛	2⅞

Resources

Le Rouvray offers a mail-order service.

To order Le Rouvray's selection of toile de Jouy fabrics or to order the pillow kit (page 7), write or fax an inquiry to us:

Le Rouvray
1, Rue Frédéric Sauton
75005 Paris
France

Fax: 43-25-51-61

(From the United States, dial 011-331 first, then the remaining numbers; from other countries, check with your local telephone operator.)

Meet the Authors

Diane de Obaldia is an "American in Paris," married to a renowned French playwright.

She is the owner and founder of Le Rouvray, the shop that is considered the mecca of quilting in France. She is also a pioneer, at the origin of the still-growing movement that put quilting "on the map" in France.

Le Rouvray began as an antique shop in a historic farm in Normandy but soon moved to Paris. An exhibit of antique quilts, belonging to Diane and sponsored by the American Embassy in Paris, toured France for two years. Through this exhibit, Le Rouvray became known throughout the country.

Cosabeth Parriaud, Diane de Obaldia, and Marie-Christine Flocard

Today, Le Rouvray is celebrating twenty years of existence at its same Left Bank (Rive Gauche) address across the Seine River from Notre Dame cathedral.

Diane's motto: "A quilt is a piece of a dream . . . stitched by hand!"

Marie-Christine Flocard was born and raised in France.

She became a quilt teacher after a career as an elementary school teacher. It was while she and her physicist husband were living in San Francisco that she began quilting with Roberta Horton. She now lives near Versailles, not far from Jouy en Josas, which is famous for its fabrics called "toiles de Jouy." She has become a toile de Jouy expert through her research done while coordinating a national exhibit of patchwork made with these fabrics. She teaches quilting at Le Rouvray and serves on the board of directors of "l'Association Française du Patchwork" (the largest French quilters' guild). Her husband and two children have been tremendously supportive of her quilting passion.

Cosabeth Parriaud was born in Brazzaville, Congo, Africa, of a French family.

She lived the first ten years of her life in four different countries! After English studies at the Sorbonne in Paris, she moved to California to perfect her English. She fell in love with quilting and worked in a quilt shop in San Francisco for two years before returning to France. For the past fourteen years, she has planned and directed the quilting classes at Le Rouvray in addition to teaching in France and internationally. Her quilts have appeared in major French women's magazines, such as *Figaro Madame*, *Elle*, and *Marie Claire Idées*. She is known for her dynamic, contemporary quilts. When she is not preparing a quilt for exhibition or one that has been commissioned, her husband and two young children keep her busy.

Embroider center
with satin stitch.

Stem stitches

Block #10 A, T
Wild Rose
(Eglantine)
Needle-turn Technique

Block #7 A, T
Anthurium
(Anthurium)
Needle-turn Technique

Flower Templates

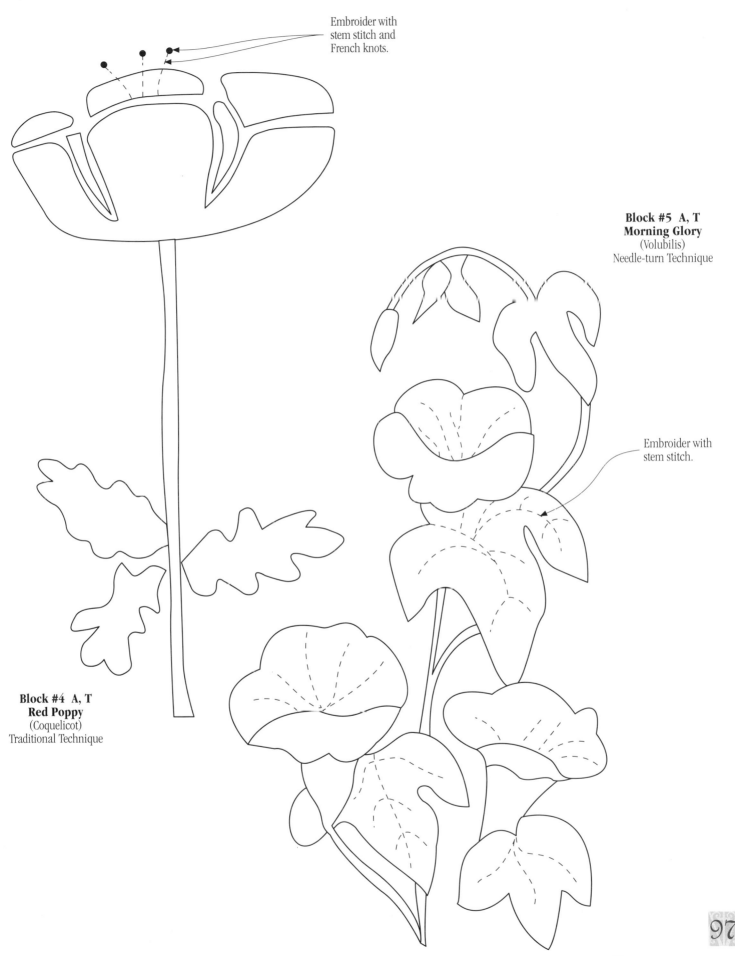

Embroider with
stem stitch and
French knots.

Block #5 A, T
Morning Glory
(Volubilis)
Needle-turn Technique

Embroider with
stem stitch.

Block #4 A, T
Red Poppy
(Coquelicot)
Traditional Technique

Flower Templates

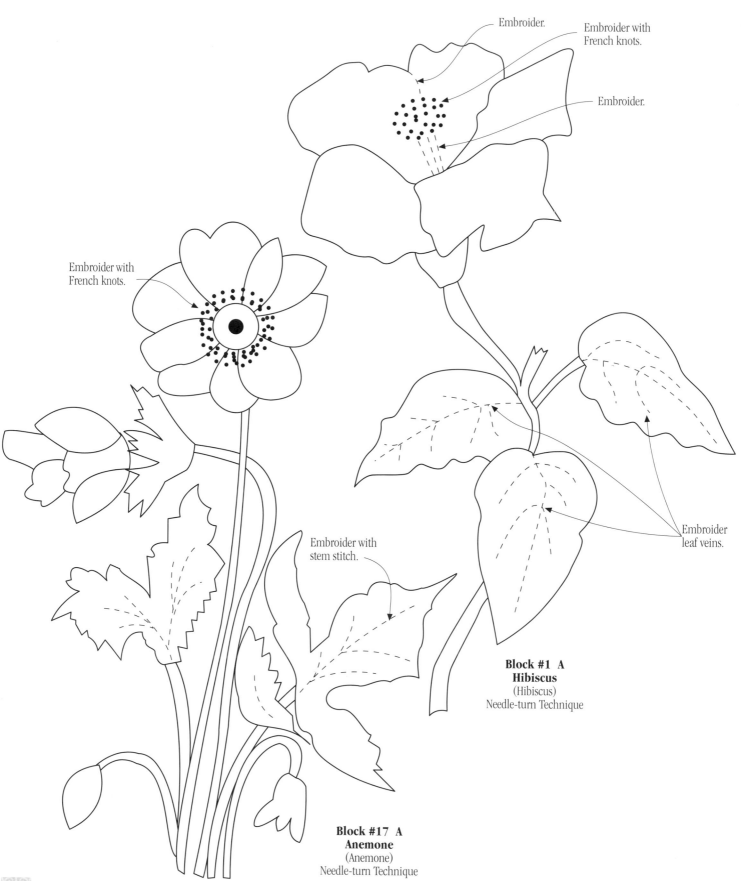

Embroider.

Embroider with
French knots.

Embroider.

Embroider with
French knots.

Embroider
leaf veins.

Embroider with
stem stitch.

Block #1 A
Hibiscus
(Hibiscus)
Needle-turn Technique

Block #17 A
Anemone
(Anemone)
Needle-turn Technique

Flower Templates

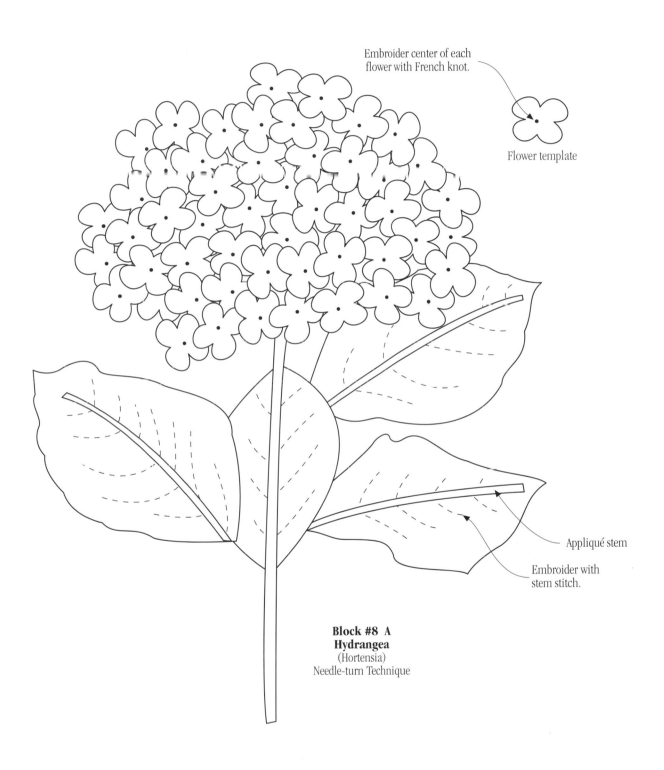

Embroider center of each
flower with French knot.

Flower template

Appliqué stem

Embroider with
stem stitch.

Block #8 A
Hydrangea
(Hortensia)
Needle-turn Technique

Flower Templates

That Patchwork Place Publications and Products

BOOKS

All the Blocks Are Geese by Mary Sue Suit
Angle Antics by Mary Hickey
Animas Quilts by Jackie Robinson
Appliqué Borders: An Added Grace by Jeana Kimball
Appliquilt: Whimsical One-Step Appliqué by Tonee White
Baltimore Bouquets by Mimi Dietrich
Bargello Quilts by Marge Edie
Basket Garden by Mary Hickey
Biblical Blocks by Rosemary Makhan
Blockbuster Quilts by Margaret J. Miller
Botanical Wreaths by Laura M. Reinstatler
Calendar Quilts by Joan Hanson
Cathedral Window: A Fresh Look by Nancy J. Martin
The Cat's Meow by Janet Kime
Colourwash Quilts by Deirdre Amsden
Corners in the Cabin by Paulette Peters
Country Medallion Sampler by Carol Doak
Country Threads by Connie Tesene and Mary Tendall
Designing Quilts by Suzanne Hammond
Easy Machine Paper Piecing by Carol Doak
Easy Quilts...By Jupiter!® by Mary Beth Maison
Fantasy Flowers by Doreen Cronkite Burbank
Five- and Seven-Patch Blocks & Quilts for the ScrapSaver
    by Judy Hopkins
Four-Patch Blocks & Quilts for the ScrapSaver
    by Judy Hopkins
Fun with Fat Quarters by Nancy J. Martin
Go Wild with Quilts by Margaret Rolfe
Handmade Quilts by Mimi Dietrich
Happy Endings by Mimi Dietrich
The Heirloom Quilt by Yolande Filson and Roberta Przybylski
Holiday Happenings by Christal Carter
In The Beginning by Sharon Evans Yenter
Irma's Sampler by Irma Eskes
Jacket Jazz by Judy Murrah
Jacket Jazz Encore by Judy Murrah
Le Rouvray by Diane de Obaldia, with
    Marie-Christine Flocard and Cosabeth Parriaud
Lessons in Machine Piecing by Marsha McCloskey
Little Quilts by Alice Berg, Sylvia Johnson, and
    Mary Ellen Von Holt
Lively Little Logs by Donna McConnell
Loving Stitches by Jeana Kimball
Make Room for Quilts by Nancy J. Martin
Nifty Ninepatches by Carolann M. Palmer
Nine-Patch Blocks & Quilts for the ScrapSaver by Judy Hopkins

Not Just Quilts by Jo Parrott
Oh! Christmas Trees compiled by Barbara Weiland
On to Square Two by Marsha McCloskey
Osage County Quilt Factory by Virginia Robertson
Our Pieceful Village by Lynn Rice
Painless Borders by Sally Schneider
A Perfect Match by Donna Lynn Thomas
Picture Perfect Patchwork by Naomi Norman
Piecemakers® Country Store by the Piecemakers
Pineapple Passion by Nancy Smith and Lynda Milligan
A Pioneer Doll and Her Quilts by Mary Hickey
Pioneer Storybook Quilts by Mary Hickey
Prairie People—Cloth Dolls to Make and Cherish by
    Marji Hadley and J. Dianne Ridgley
Quick & Easy Quiltmaking by Mary Hickey, Nancy J. Martin,
    Marsha McCloskey and Sara Nephew
The Quilted Apple by Laurene Sinema
Quilted for Christmas compiled by Ursula Reikes
The Quilters' Companion compiled by That Patchwork Place
The Quilting Bee by Jackie Wolff and Lori Aluna
Quilting Makes the Quilt by Lee Cleland
Quilts for All Seasons by Christal Carter
Quilts for Baby: Easy as A, B, C by Ursula Reikes
Quilts for Kids by Carolann M. Palmer
Quilts from Nature by Joan Colvin
Quilts to Share by Janet Kime
Red Wagon Originals by Gerry Kimmel and Linda Brannock
Rotary Riot by Judy Hopkins and Nancy J. Martin
Rotary Roundup by Judy Hopkins and Nancy J. Martin
Round About Quilts by J. Michelle Watts
Round Robin Quilts by Pat Magaret and Donna Slusser
Samplings from the Sea by Rosemary Makhan
ScrapMania by Sally Schneider
Sensational Settings by Joan Hanson
Sewing on the Line by Lesly-Claire Greenberg
Shortcuts: A Concise Guide to Rotary Cutting
    by Donna Lynn Thomas (French, Dutch,
    Japanese, and metric versions available)
Shortcuts Sampler by Roxanne Carter
Shortcuts to the Top by Donna Lynn Thomas
Small Talk by Donna Lynn Thomas
Smoothstitch® Quilts by Roxi Eppler
The Stitchin' Post by Jean Wells and Lawry Thorn
Strips That Sizzle by Margaret J. Miller
Sunbonnet Sue All Through the Year by Sue Linker
Tea Party Time by Nancy J. Martin
Template-Free® Quiltmaking by Trudie Hughes
Template-Free® Quilts and Borders by Trudie Hughes
Template-Free® Stars by Jo Parrott
Two for Your Money by Jo Parrott
Watercolor Quilts by Pat Magaret and Donna Slusser

VIDEO Shortcuts to America's Best-Loved Quilts

TOOLS

4", 6", 8", and metric Bias Square®

BiRangle™	Ruby Beholder™
Pineapple Rule	ScrapMaster
Rotary Rule™	Rotary Mate™

Many titles are available at your local quilt shop. For more information, send $2 for a color catalog to That Patchwork Place, Inc., PO Box 118, Bothell WA 98041-0118 USA.

☎ Call 1-800-426-3126 for the name and location of the quilt shop nearest you.